Psychology Revivals

Football in its Place

In the late 1980s football was in a state of crisis. Falling attendances and a genuine unease among potential spectators about going to live football matches suggested that, without radical changes, the game would soon become a minority spectator sport. Originally published in 1989, reissued now with a new preface, *Football in its Place* presented a new approach to the problem that concentrates on the spectators' experience of football and on the places where it is played.

This approach recognizes four themes, which relate directly to the spectators' experience: spectator comfort; the need for effective crowd control; the problems of coping in emergencies; and variations in club cultures. A special chapter on football-related violence shows how this needs to be understood in relation to all of these themes and not treated as a problem in isolation. This was said to be the only way to reverse the spiral that had given rise to hooliganism.

Finally, the authors discuss the options for the future on football. They emphasize that football is a recreational activity whose management should be treated as part of the leisure industry. All aspects of the game, its traditions, club variations and heritage, needed to be harnessed if football was again to be Britain's most popular spectator sport. Today we can see the impact that the points made in this book have contributed to how we continue to watch and enjoy football now.

Football in its Place
An Environmental Psychology of Football Grounds

David Canter, Miriam Comber
and David L. Uzzell

LONDON AND NEW YORK

First published in 1989
by Routledge

This edition first published in 2024 by Routledge
4 Park Square, Milton Park, Abingdon, Oxon, OX14 4RN

and by Routledge
605 Third Avenue, New York, NY 10017

Routledge is an imprint of the Taylor & Francis Group, an informa business

© 1989 David Canter, Miriam Comber and David L. Uzzell

All rights reserved. No part of this book may be reprinted or reproduced or utilised in any form or by any electronic, mechanical, or other means, now known or hereafter invented, including photocopying and recording, or in any information storage or retrieval system, without permission in writing from the publishers.

Publisher's Note
The publisher has gone to great lengths to ensure the quality of this reprint but points out that some imperfections in the original copies may be apparent.

Disclaimer
The publisher has made every effort to trace copyright holders and welcomes correspondence from those they have been unable to contact.

ISBN: 978-1-032-77228-8 (hbk)
ISBN: 978-1-003-48257-4 (ebk)
ISBN: 978-1-032-77346-9 (pbk)

Book DOI 10.4324/9781003482574

NEW PREFACE TO THE 2024 REISSUE

In 1989, when the book was first published, football was in crisis. The numbers attending football over the previous two decades had dropped steadily to be two thirds of what they had been when England hosted the World Cup in 1966. Over the previous decade the number of acts of violence and arrests, both inside and outside football stadia, had risen steadily. The terrible state of British football came to a head when a fire took hold of the stands at Bradford City's Valley Parade ground on 11th May 1985. Fifty-six spectators were killed and 265 injured. This led to the establishment of the Popplewell *Inquiry into Crowd Safety at Sports Grounds.* Soon after Sir Oliver Popplewell started work, a crowd crush at Heysel Stadium, in Brussels on 29th May 1985, resulted in 39 deaths and 400 injuries. More people were dying in football ground disasters than in the whole of major, potentially dangerous industries, such as Steel and Petrochemical.

By that point, I had been carrying out studies for a decade of behaviour in emergencies and safety in industry. Aware of this, Sir Oliver invited me to meet him and offer views on the issues relating to these disasters. As a social scientist my immediate reaction was to tell him at that meeting that a study of football supporters was necessary. I suggested that there was a culture within football, a set of attitudes similar to those that caused accidents in heavy industries, or the management of risk in domestic and working environments, which needed to be understood and dealt with.

To my surprise, Sir Oliver thought this was a good idea. There and then, he asked me how much such a study would cost. I pulled a figure out. He turned to his civil servant and asked if such funds were available. They were. I was therefore commissioned on the spot! A unique moment in my career as an applied psychologist. Then Sir Oliver told me that my report would need to be completed before the start of the 1985/86 football season, September 1985. It was early Summer. No football games were being played. I therefore had to find a way of getting access to football supporters out of season. The idea came up of approaching people near football grounds to see if they were supporters. That enabled data to be collected from a thousand people across ten clubs that varied in size, wealth, league position and location. The results of that study provided the basis for *Football in its Place*.

Not having any great knowledge or interest in football, I was fortunate in having a colleague in David Uzzell. He is not only passionate about football but also shares my academic commitment to environmental psychology. This recognises that human activity interacts with its surroundings to give shape to experiences of places. That it in turn feeds back into what people expect to occur in those places. Miriam Comber, another social psychologist colleague, well-versed in handling data and statistics, was also available to help us manage such a large study in so short a time.

Our results made clear that football was in crisis because it was not being managed as part of the entertainment industry. It was increasingly becoming a haven for aggression and the kind of macho culture in which discomfort and violence were creating an alienating culture. Families and women, as well as men who just wanted to enjoy watching the game, were being driven away from the stadium because of how unappealing the experience was. This was producing a distillation process that increased the destructive culture. The book documents the details of these findings, coming to the conclusion that if there were not radical change even greater disasters would occur. After our report was submitted to the Popplewell Inquiry, on 15th April 1989, the disaster occurred at Hillsborough football ground in which 97 people were killed and 766 injured.

A particularly stark illustration of our pessimistic prediction was that early in 1989 the graphic designer for our book chose a photograph for the cover taken on 30th April 1978, at The Dell, Southampton's football ground. A week or two after this cover was available in bookstores the disaster at Hillsborough occurred, generating photographs horrifically similar to our cover photograph.

Lord Justice Taylor set up an inquiry into the Hillsborough disaster, asking to meet me. I reiterated the findings of our study, emphasising the environmental psychology perspective that the terraces on which people typically stand to watch football, whilst not inherently dangerous, contributed to the destructive culture that was destroying football. This was part of the argument that caused him to propose having all-seater stadiums.

It is with some satisfaction, when watching football crowds nowadays, to see how many families and women are present, part of a friendly enjoyable atmosphere. I like to think that *Football in its Place* contributed to that resurgence in the spirit of watching football.

David Canter
December 2023

ORIGINAL COVER FROM 1989

FOOTBALL IN ITS PLACE

An environmental psychology of football grounds

DAVID CANTER, MIRIAM COMBER,
AND DAVID L. UZZELL

ROUTLEDGE
London and New York

First published 1989
by Routledge
11 New Fetter Lane, London EC4P 4EE
29 West 35th Street, New York, NY 10001

© 1989 David Canter, Miriam Comber, and David L. Uzzell

Phototypeset by Input Typesetting Ltd, London SW19 8DR

Printed and bound in Great Britain by
Biddles, Guildford and Kings Lynn

All rights reserved. No part of this book may be
reprinted or reproduced or utilized in any form or
by any electronic, mechanical, or other means, now
known or hereafter invented, including photocopying
and recording, or in any information storage or
retrieval system, without permission in writing from
the publishers.

British Library Cataloguing in Publication Data

Canter, David, *1944–*
Football in its place : an environmental
psychology of football grounds
1. Great Britain. Association football
supporters. Behaviour. Environmental factors
I. Title II. Comber, Miriam III. Uzzell,
David L. (David Lawrence), *1951–*
306'.483

ISBN 0-415-01240-6

CONTENTS

List of tables and figures	vii
Foreword by Sir Oliver Popplewell	xi
Introduction: background and beginnings	xiii
1 FOUR THEMES	1
2 SPECTATORS' VIEWS	22
3 CLUB CULTURES	57
4 CROWDS AND EMERGENCIES	86
5 COPING WITH VIOLENCE	103
6 THE FINAL SCORE	127
Notes	166
Index	170

TABLES AND FIGURES

Figure 1.1　Total Football League attendances over the past 24 years.　x

Figure 1.2　Ratio of total arrests per 10,000 spectators, inside and outside the ground, over the past 10 years.　x

Figure 2.1　Percentage of yes and no answers to the question: "Do/did you go regularly to the ground?"　27

Figure 2.2　Percentage responses to the question: "How often do/did you go to the ground?"　28

Figure 2.3　Percentage who watched their team last season.　29

Figure 2.4　Comparison of the percentage of lapsed and regular supporters who said they went to most games, at each of ten clubs.　33

Figure 2.5　Comparison of the percentage of lapsed and regular supporters who said it was all right to share the home ground, at each of ten clubs.　34

Figure 2.6　Comparison of the percentage of lapsed and regular supporters who said an enjoyable game was more important than winning, at each of ten clubs.　35

Figure 2.7　Comparison of the percentage of lapsed and regular supporters who said "it's all right to take the mickey", at each of ten clubs.　36

Figure 2.8　Comparisons of the proportions worried about safety at home and away matches, at each of ten clubs.　39

Figure 2.9　Comparisons of the socio-economic status of those who sit and those who stand – percentages of classes A, B, C1.　43

Figure 2.10　Percentages of those who sit and those who stand who agree that an enjoyable game is more important than winning.　44

Figure 2.11	Percentages of those who sit and those who stand who agree that "I wouldn't be as critical of physical violence at a football match as I would be in other situations".	45
Figure 2.12	Percentages of those who sit and those who stand who agree that "It's all right to take the mickey out of other sides' football supporters".	46
Figure 2.13	Percentages of those who sit and those who stand who would pay more for better facilities.	47
Figure 2.14	Percentages of respondents, at each of ten clubs, who watch other teams and percentages who support membership schemes.	50
Table 2.1	Teams watched by more than 3 per cent of each club's supporters	52
Figure 2.15	Percentages of respondents, at each of ten clubs, who go/went to most matches who agree/disagree with membership card schemes.	53
Figure 2.16	Percentages of respondents, at each of ten clubs, who agree with the statement: "It's all right to take the mickey out of other sides' football supporters", who agree/disagree with membership card schemes.	54
Figure 2.17	Percentages of respondents, at each of ten clubs, who think it would be worth paying a little more if facilities at the ground were better, who agree/disagree with membership card schemes.	55
Figure 3.1	Percentages of respondents who go to most games, compared across ten clubs.	59
Figure 3.2	Percentages of respondents who go to away games, at each of ten clubs.	60
Figure 3.3	Percentages of respondents who hold season tickets, at each of ten clubs.	61
Figure 3.4	Percentages of respondents who have seen their team play abroad, at each of ten clubs.	62
Figure 3.5	Percentages of respondents who normally stand, at each of ten clubs.	65
Table 3.1	Ratings given to the physical conditions at each ground	66
Figure 3.6	Percentages of respondents who think the ground is comfortable, at each of ten clubs.	67
Figure 3.7	Percentages of respondents who think conditions are above average, at each of ten clubs.	68

Figure 3.8	Percentages of respondents who think that improvements are needed, at each of ten clubs.	69
Figure 3.9	Percentages of respondents who agreed that they heard a lot of obscene language, and percentages who were worried by any bad language, at each of ten clubs.	71
Figure 3.10	Percentages of respondents who agree "there are a lot of racist shouts or chants", and who agree "the racist shouts or chants do worry me", at each of ten clubs.	73
Table 3.2	Percentage of regular supporters from the ten clubs agreeing with each of three statements	77
Table 4.1	Sequence of events at Bradford City football ground fire	99

Figure 1.1: Total Football League attendances over the past 24 years.

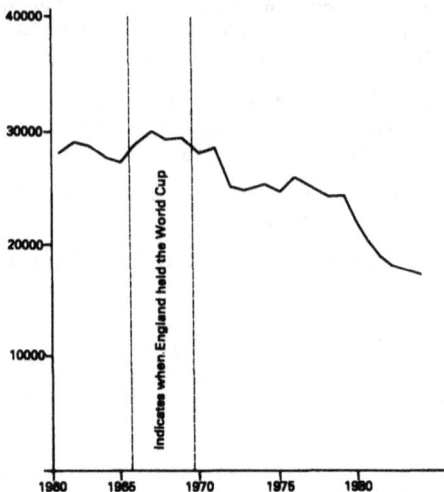

Note: Overall attendances at football league matches over the 24 years from 1961 to 1985 have dropped from the peak of around 29 million in the late sixties, when England held the world cup, to around 18 million in recent years. The attendances have fallen off most steeply from the beginning of the eighties.

Figure 1.2: Ratio of total arrests per 10,000 spectators, inside and outside the ground, over the past 10 years.

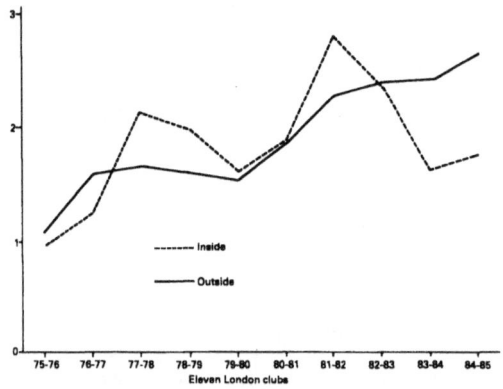

Note: Ratio of total arrests per 10,000 spectators, inside and outside football grounds of eleven London football clubs over the ten years from 1975 to 1985. The steady increase in arrests outside grounds is apparent despite the variation in arrests within the grounds. This variation relates to legislation in the early seventies (applying to first division clubs), and the late seventies (applying to other clubs), requiring stricter controls on football grounds. The legislation was brought in as a result of major incidents at football matches.

FOREWORD
by
Sir Oliver Popplewell

When I was asked to conduct the enquiry into the fire disaster at Bradford and the outbreak of violence in the Leeds–Birmingham match, I had little or no knowledge of the psychology of football. Happily David Canter was invited to provide and did provide me with a wealth of evidence on all aspects of the game which was a major contribution to our understanding of the problems confronting football.

This book is a comprehensive work which deserves to be read and digested not only by fellow researchers, but by a wider public audience which has an interest in the game of football. There is no subject upon which people talk with such confidence and so little knowledge, or where the gap between fact and fiction is so great.

As David Canter points out the strands which go to make up the fabric of football are many and varied. There is the interrelation of the spectators with their differing backgrounds and separate environments; of the grounds with differing facilities and separate histories; of the management varying in quality and outlook; of the players contributing through their skill and behaviour to reaction on the terraces; of the police whose handling of problems is fundamental to the exercising of control; and of the government intervening only in moments of crisis (what David Canter calls regulation by crisis).

All these factors affect the psychology of the game. It is a particularly interesting statistic that spectators generally think their ground is comfortable or quite comfortable. I confess that when standing

FOREWORD

on the terraces in the rain on a Wednesday evening in February during my enquiry I did not share that view. Perhaps I would have made a poor statistic. But facts and figures are important in any "in depth" enquiry in this field and they are well deployed.

The scientific approach adopted in this book lays bare the myths with which we are fed by the media. The subject of hooliganism is a constant topic for discussion, with instant remedies and wild headlines. Historically the matter is put in perspective. Remedies are suggested which the authorities would do well to heed. If past experience is anything to go by, they will not. There is one worrying statistic relating to the numbers of police required every week not just inside the ground but in the town both before and after the game and in the elaborate military-style planning at a higher level which is involved throughout the year.

One question which needs to be asked is whether such an enormous expenditure of police resources can any longer be justified simply to enable a minute proportion of the community to attend a function run by a private organization for profit. During my enquiry we were told that, in one county, between one third and one half of the whole police force was deployed on a Saturday afternoon when there was a football match on. How long can this situation continue?

One club we visited (who shall be nameless) had however cured their hooligan problem. On the first occasion of trouble the spectator was put out of the ground. On the second occasion he was brought back in and forced to watch the game!

No one however could be bored with this excellent and well researched book and it is a major contribution to the subject. It gives me great pleasure to have been invited to write the foreword.

INTRODUCTION: BACKGROUND AND BEGINNINGS

Duas tantum res anxius optat, panem et circenses
(He longs for only two things – bread and the big match)
Juvenal, *Of the Citizen these Days*, circa AD100

HERITAGE AND BEYOND

The world's most popular team sport, football, grew out of medieval village mêlées in which two groups struggled with each other to move a leather-covered bladder to a place defended by their opponents. Many different local groups took part, perhaps the most intriguing being the annual match between the married women and the spinsters of Cross of Scone in Scotland, in which the spinsters, it seems, were usually badly defeated.

These mêlées tended to happen as major communal events on annual feast days, most usually on Shrove Tuesday, which was then a day of festival before a fast. So, the occurence of the major national football finals in the early spring, places them quite close in the calendar to their archaic forebears.

The exuberant social qualities of these mediaeval festivities did, also, at times go beyond the limits the authorities were prepared to tolerate. One of the earliest documented annual games, played in Chester and possibly dating back to Roman times, was stopped in the Middle Ages because it had become so violent; it was replaced with a running match. Yet the interest in these communal competitions grew, so that by 1365 Edward III prohibited football because he feared it was distracting youth from pastimes seen as being of more military importance, such as archery.

INTRODUCTION

However, what is particularly noteworthy about the early contests, out of which present-day football grew, is that they were very firmly located in both a community and a physical location. Indeed for many centuries the rules of the games played were so specific to the particular village and the particular places in which they were played that matches between groups from different areas were virtually unknown. Thus on the famous occasion in 1823, when William Webb Ellis, contrary to local rules, carried the ball in a game at Rugby school, thereby inventing Rugby football, his actions were merely characteristic of the confusions of the day, when it was still not established whether the ball could be handled or not.

It was only with the evolution of different types of football and the codification of the rules in the mid-nineteenth century that games between teams from different localities became possible. As a consequence, the game changed from being essentially a parochial pastime. It had unfolded according to local possibilities and predilections, in which the young and active of the community could all take part. It now became the special preserve of a team that could represent the community in competition with those from other places. Thus spectators and players became distinct.

With the advent of professional football there was an obvious need to create special places in which spectators could watch and where teams could play on a reliable pitch. This brought a further stage in the separation from each other of the various groups involved in football. It also started the distancing of the football club from the local community out of which it had grown. Where originally a village would take part in an annual festival, there developed the management, training and organisation of a specially selected group of individuals to take part in a competition of more importance for its national than for its local significance.

Of especial significance is the way this development generates a new class of performer in the football enterprise: the paying spectator. Yet the basic organisation of football is built around what happens on the field of play. The team manager, like the theatrical director, is seen as the most significant figure. But the theatre has had centuries of development that has lead to a great variety of different building forms, and the development of an astute understanding of how to woo the audience. At many footballing events in Britain it is still possible to feel that you are little removed from the medieval days, when you might have stood on a hill overlooking

INTRODUCTION

the village green watching the spinsters try to force a leather-covered bladder past the married women of the parish. The important difference, though, is that it is not your village, your sister is not amongst the players and you have been charged half a day's pay to stand in the rain and watch.

The most important message to take from this potted history of football is that players and spectators, managers and supporters and all the other different groups associated with professional football, have come into existence because of the way football has developed from its very early origins as a team game into its present status as a major spectator sport. The fragmentation this has produced is at the heart of the problems football faces as a commercial enterprise. It is the very existence of these different groups, removed from their community and from their followers, that makes the study of the present-day experience of football, and the places in which it is played, so important.

The shouts and jeers that are expected in a football crowd, the terraces and the pie stalls, the team heroes and mascots, scarves and banners, are all a natural part of its origins in village mêlées. But as so often happens, it can take decades, or even centuries, for a popular activity to change its nature to accommodate changes in the society around it. It is often only when there is some sort of public outcry that the pressures build up for a radical re-examination of activities previously taken for granted. In writing this book we think that football is reaching the point at which it will be able to respond to the necessary reappraisals.

We believe that the source for such appraisals is in a close consideration of the actual experience of going to a football match. This experience is linked to a particular set of activities and a specific location, which provides a secondary focus for the book.

We will use our focus on football to illustrate the contributions of a perspective that studies the human implications of the physical environment. This approach, known as *environmental psychology*, has matured over the past few years through an examination of buildings such as hospitals, offices, schools and the wider environment. Only recently have environmental psychologists begun to look at more informal places – settings for leisure activities. Football stadia, then, do provide an interesting context in which to explore further this approach.

INTRODUCTION

READY TO RESPOND

The primary reason why professional football may now respond to an environmental psychological analysis is that it has received a great deal of media attention over the last few seasons, usually because of failings in the way it has been managed or its spectators have behaved. A few social scientists have acknowledged this attention and recognised that the terraces provide a rich field for research.[1]

As seems inevitable these days, like much social science research, the research agenda is indirectly set by politicians and the media. The research that is the focus of this book is in that tradition. It emanated from a request from Sir Oliver Popplewell to provide evidence for his Committee of Inquiry into Crowd Safety and Control at Sports Grounds.[2] This was set up in the aftermath of the disastrous events of the early summer of 1985 when fire broke out at Bradford City Football Club, a wall collapsed at the Birmingham City ground and fighting between fans in Heysel Stadium led to many deaths. Yet from our initial contacts with the official inquiry it became clear to us that there was a need to examine our national sport with a broader perspective than that provided in dealing directly with those tragic events.

We are aware that present-day professional football, like all other uses of particular places, is founded on a mixture of frequently contradictory objectives. We are also aware that the divisions we have outlined between players, managers and spectators provide an implicit challenge to the view that opinions on football are the prerogative of the spokesmen of the football associations. We posed the question as to what the public, the spectators, think about football and the facilities at football grounds. We argue that the future of football must lie with its consumers and that it is to them that we should turn for a fuller understanding of the predicaments it faces.

Our investigations posed a number of questions: What, for example, do spectators think about the facilities at football grounds? Are they comfortable during matches? What sort of event or occasion are spectators looking for when they go to a football match? What is the typical experience of visiting a football ground? Do they feel safe from violence or accidents? Where in the ground is safest? How racist is the crowd and do political groups provoke violence? And

INTRODUCTION

what of lapsed supporters, those people who were regular visitors to grounds until a year or so ago, but who have now stopped attending? Who are these people? Why did they withdraw their support? Are their perceptions of football and the football experience different from those of supporters still attending?

A PSYCHOLOGICAL VIEW

We came to this book not essentially as journalists or football enthusiasts (although we have and do play both roles on occasion) but as psychologists. We see ourselves as scientists armed with theories and methods that allow us to explore the social and environmental processes that structure human actions and experiences. It has been our concern to set our analysis and comments within an essentially social and environmental psychological framework. Because environmental psychology is the study of how people relate to and interact with their environment, it is especially applicable to an investigation of human behaviour in a clearly defined type of place such as a sports stadium. Issues ranging from the siting of crush barriers and the optimum width of exits to the symbolism of having fans segregated into recognisable territories are all part of the domain of environmental psychology. Environmental psychology also draws heavily on its older cousin, social psychology. This has been addressing issues such as group polarisation, stereotyping, segregation and competitiveness for over half a century now. There is also much we already know about changing attitudes and behaviour, the discussion of which must be at the centre of any informed policy for the future of British football.

In order to develop our argument and acquire evidence that would test and illustrate it, several sources of information have been used. Accounts of all incidents at football matches, in Britain and overseas, which have occurred since 1972 were examined. These include fire emergencies, walls collapsing and violent incidents. In some cases, such as the Bradford fire and the collapse of a wall at Birmingham City, very detailed information was available. In other cases, however, there has been very little documentation of the incident.

We were also able to spend some time with the Fulham division of the Metropolitan Police. Through their friendly and instructive co-operation we were able to observe in detail the preparation for,

INTRODUCTION

and policing of, matches. Naturally, this also involved discussions with the police and with many people involved in the management and control of the games. We are very grateful to all concerned for their kind and willing help.

The Red Cross and the St John Ambulance Brigade also kindly let us have their figures for casualties at football matches, which include both injuries caused by violence and the types of casualty which may occur at any large gathering of people, such as other large sports, leisure or political events. These statistics were used in conjunction with figures on arrests to give an outline picture of the extent of disorder at various matches. To these two organisations we also wish to record our thanks.

THE SURVEY

An examination of emergencies that have occurred in public places and the patterns of behaviour associated with them gives an essentially objective, external account of actions in stressful, dangerous situations. It throws into high relief dramatic episodes and particular, extreme incidents. Yet millions of people attend hundreds of football games in Britain each year. Very, very few of these are marred by any unpleasant incidents at all. But the objective facts are not what influences people's actions. It is their understanding and interpretation of the facts that is significant to them. So, we considered it important to get at least a glimpse of spectators' own views on safety and conditions at the grounds they visit.

Our largest single source of information was a survey which canvassed the views of nearly 1,000 supporters at ten clubs across the United Kingdom in both the Football League and the Scottish League. The survey and its findings are central to later chapters. The views and experience of supporters are obviously important and yet often ignored. We owe a special debt of gratitude to the Popplewell Inquiry for recognising the importance of the spectators' perspective and so supporting our survey.

Finally, and not unimportantly, we have been attending football matches for over twenty years. It would be difficult not to stand on the terraces without looking at the spectators, place and activities through professional eyes as psychologists. This has necessarily contributed to our perceptions and conclusions.

Chapter One

FOUR THEMES

WHAT IS FOOTBALL'S PLACE?

In our title for this book we draw attention to the need to think about where professional football happens – not just its physical location, although we are giving that much more attention than it usually receives, but we are also considering its place in the lives of its supporters and in the community that houses it.

We know that the title to this book is ambiguous. It could imply that we wish to put football firmly in some obscure place that many may argue it deserves. Or our title could, with equal force, suggest that professional football should be given the pride of place that would reflect its significance. Our argument is that the problems that beset British football could lead in either direction. If it is to grow in a positive direction, then, it is essential to understand what prospects its environment – its social and physical context – has to offer.

Four Themes

The place of football, then, includes the concrete and metal that make up football stadia and house the grounds and their facilities. It includes the location of those facilities within the metropolitan or urban community. But, more importantly, it includes the perception and attitudes of those who support, or might support, football, the position they assign the game and their experience of watching it. A better understanding of spectators' views is, therefore, one of the themes of our study.

A second theme is that each football club evolves its own culture.

FOOTBALL IN ITS PLACE

This derives from recognising that when looking at the location of football in a community of interested parties such as supporters and managers, or in a physical community such as Chelsea or Everton, there will be important differences between and within those communities. These different cultures need to be taken account of in discussing what actions should be taken and by whom.

The challenge of football comes in its ability to attract regularly large crowds of people. It is therefore also typically positioned in people's minds next to considerations about the behaviour of large crowds and the need to manage them. This aspect of the particular qualities of the experience of watching football requires special consideration and so forms the essence of the third theme to our book.

When football crowds contain violent elements, the particular physical qualities of a crowded football stadium and the place that football takes in people's minds create a powerful combination. A negative spiral of thoughts and actions may then be set in motion. Football is shunted into a corner for those who will tolerate violence, and it is difficult for it to obtain a better place thereafter. Coping with violence therefore is our fourth theme. It is not our first because the problem of the violence associated with football has to be seen as part of the general context in which football operates. If all violence were to stop at football matches we think it unlikely that football would regain all its lost supporters, but until such violence is stopped it is unlikely that football will be able to put itself on target to regain the pride of place it held in earlier years.

ENVIRONMENTAL PSYCHOLOGY

Central to our approach through the field of environmental psychology is the idea that our physical surroundings are relevant to our actions and well-being, but usually not in any clear and direct way. It is the unravelling of these indirect processes that makes this such a difficult yet important topic for study.

Many of the processes that can be seen operating in football can also be seen in many other places of public entertainment in other areas of our cities. So, in focusing on football, we can touch on themes of a more general kind as well and perhaps help prevent other sports, like cricket or rugby, from drifting the way of football.

FOUR THEMES

Many of the principles that emerge when considering football are also very useful for looking at other socially important issues.

Before considering some of the general principles of environmental psychology, however, it is necessary to emphasise that despite the general relevance of the study of football grounds, there is one special difficulty in writing about football and its place in our lives and communities: many, many more people have seen snippets of football matches on television than have ever been to a football match. Although only 1 in 20 men go to a football match within any given month, 2 out of 3 British men watch a football match on television in that time. Further, even though it is less than 1 in 100 women who go to a football match in a month, half of all British women admit to having watched a match on television during that time.[1]

A major international match may be seen on television by at least 1 in 3 of the population. 23.7 million people in Britain watched England play Argentina in the 1986 World Cup. The World Cup final is probably seen by 1 person in 5 of the population of the world. Football is as much a central part of the culture of our global village as James Bond and Coca Cola. Its major heroes, whether it was Stanley Matthews, Dixie Dean, Bobby Charlton or Pele in the past, Lineker or Diego Marradonna now, have a following that politicians aspire to and salaries of which even barristers can only dream. So, most of us *think* we know about football from the highly diluted, indirect yet vivid accounts we have had of it.

The professional accounts of football present a complementary problem to the researcher. The people who write about football (and many of the people who have studied it) are enthusiasts. Their views are inevitably coloured by their own particular desires for the game. So, if we want to throw any new light on the problems British football is facing it is essential to disentangle the many threads that come together at and around football matches. Most importantly, we must try to establish some scientific principles on which to base our considerations. Otherwise the discussion will continue on the basis of opinion and supposition with vested interest distorting the argument.

In the usual public debate particular aspects of the problem are highlighted by specific incidents. Then, general myths that grow from saloon bar discussions are used to elaborate those ideas. Further, there is no evidence that the central authorities of international football work any more systematically in coming to their conclusions. Newspaper outrage appears, on occasion, to be enough to stimulate rapid reaction such as the banning of British teams from European competition.

Our approach is rather different to this. We have tried to consider football as an aspect of human behaviour and experience in a particular type of place. This has enabled us to draw upon a scientific, psychological approach. This has a number of distinguishing characteristics.

First of all, a scientific psychological analysis attempts to work with forms of explanation that are drawn from as clear a definition as possible of what the various constituents mean. It also attempts to provide a logically consistent account of the relationships between the various constituents. So, the notion of a crowd or a hooligan is not taken as having an obvious incontrovertible meaning. Instead, an attempt is made to be as clear as possible as to how these terms are being used and what they are being taken to mean. In the present book we shall try to avoid the often pedantic style that is almost inevitable when a full scientific discourse of everyday matters is involved; but we will none the less endeavour to draw upon such a background and make it as clear as possible to the reader.

The second distinguishing characteristic of a psychological focus is the type of evidence on which the research scientist draws. This is usually graced with the term 'data'. What this means is that a systematic, precise and organised account of what is being used to defend the arguments and viewpoints is put forward. Wherever possible such evidence is in the publicly available domain. In other words it is not personal opinion. It may be based upon a summary of the opinions that many people hold, but in this case the summary is derived from a systematic exploration of those opinions. In this sense it is open to public view because any researcher could establish whether or not he or she would be able to obtain a similar set of opinions if approaching people in the same way.

What differentiates newspaper fact-gathering from psychological 'data' is that in the latter a large sample of people is systematically asked for its views using unbiased questions. Newspapers only ask a few people for their views, and the questions they ask will determine the answers they receive. Newspapers will report what they want to report and will select evidence to fit the story and argument they are putting forward. In this way certain groups can become

FOUR THEMES

scapegoats to feed the popular imagination. For example, if some people on the way to a football match are involved in a fight, the headlines may emphasise 'Football Hooligans in Pre-Match Fracas'. The social scientist would want to be sure that football played some significant part in the fight before giving the activity the 'football hooligan' label.

What is said in newspapers may, of course, be used as data. What witnesses say to the police or results that come from participant observation or the analysis of interview records or questionnaire responses all provide data based on views and opinions. These, however, are treated as information which is open to systematic, scientific examination and analysis. Again, the full technicalities of such analyses require a certain sophistication in statistical procedures and so we shall avoid presenting the details in the present volume. However, we will be drawing upon such analyses in developing our case.

Science, of course, like all other human endeavours is not free of error or of human foible. The difference is that the errors are identifiable. The controllable foibles are usually revealed through the course of open debate amongst scientists.

This scientific process is frequently misunderstood. The image presented in the media and often presented at school is that science is solely about the collection of 'facts'. The amassing of data is seen as being the very essence of scientific activity. This is quite mistaken, for although data are important to science, whether it be natural science or social science, the data are only a means to an end. The objective of all science is to develop systems of explanation that can be tested against the facts. In a word, science is concerned with theories. Social science develops theories about social behaviour.

It follows, therefore, that the most appropriate way of summarising the results of a number of years of environmental psychology is to give an account of the general principles that have emerged from these studies. This is much more helpful in understanding the place of football than recounting all the data that have been collected; although, as will become apparent, we did collect a substantial quantity of data to help us develop and test these ideas in the context of football.

FOOTBALL IN ITS PLACE

DIFFERING PERSPECTIVES

One of the most common findings of environmental psychological research has been the difference in perspective that different people can have on the same place. School teachers see their schools very differently from the way their pupils see them. Teachers may comment on a cramped classroom, where children will only notice a spacious playground. Architects think and talk about most buildings in ways that are different from the people who actually use those buildings. They will see the form and interplay of spaces where users will see something that is just big and draughty. Ask a keen fisherman to talk about the Norfolk Broads and contrast that with what a yachtsman tells you about the same place and you would think they are each describing completely different places.

The point about all these different viewpoints is that they complement one another. There is no definitive basis on which it is possible to say that some are right and some are wrong.

The differing views derive from different types of contact with the place. If anyone wishes to understand what the experience of watching football is all about, how it might be improved or changed, then it is not enough to discuss this with a few friends or even to ask a number of 'experts'. It is essential to question systematically a variety of different groups involved, and most importantly to reach the group whose views are least often canvassed – the spectators themselves. This type of consumer research can be remarkably revealing if carried out in an appropriate way.

We shall describe in some detail in later chapters the survey we conducted of 'lapsed' and 'regular' supporters, but it is worth noting here a few of the benefits of carrying out a survey irrespective of what is done with the results. One of them is the direct public relations value of making consumers of a service aware that the providers of the service are indeed interested in their reaction. Simply doing the survey, quite independently of its results, may therefore be beneficial.

A second benefit is that the act of carrying out such a study does reveal current understanding of who should be approached and why. Our initial overtures to some club management revealed their belief that they were already in contact with spectators through the officials of their supporters' club. This indicated to us an ignorance of the likely differences between members of the supporters' club and many other spectators.

We also found that in undertaking our particular study we became aware of the great variety of people who have an interest in what goes on in football grounds. Probably the biggest surprise here was the very large police involvement in football. It is only when you go behind the scenes, and begin to add up the numbers, that it becomes apparent that there is a huge administrative police system in existence solely to deal with football crowds. The police, of course, do have their own particular perspective as well and this is drawn upon throughout subsequent chapters.

SYMBOLIC SIGNIFICANCE

Environmental psychologists have also drawn attention to the powerful ways in which our surroundings carry implications, not so much through their direct effects on us as through the meanings they convey. Most of us can look at a place and form a view as to the type of person who might be found in that place, what they are likely to do there and why. Within these patterns of associations, judgments can be made about the status of those involved and about the nature of their involvement with the activities being carried out. A surprising variety of other informed guesses and judgments about places, the activities and people they house, is also frequently made. Let us emphasise that these judgments are not necessarily correct. They may well be systematically wrong. The important point is that they are made, frequently with great conviction, and therefore people frequently act on those judgments.

For example, consider a large industrial factory with its unrelieved concrete and iron supports, its flights of stairs leading to draughty workshops and its generally dull appearance. Contrast that with a bright supermarket full of gaily packaged goods with soft music and well-dressed staff. Now, what do you think will be typical of the people in these different settings? Their age, style, sex, how they feel about things and how they treat each other will be assumed to be different. It is even possible to show that judgments of potential inhabitants vary with quite small differences in the building details. In one study carried out many years ago, people were shown pictures of private offices and asked to guess what the people were like who used those offices.[2] It was found that the pleasantness of the possible occupant was judged to be higher if the room had a sloping ceiling rather than a flat ceiling.

Market research and consumer research organisations have long known about the possible implications of the implicit messages that the physical environment carries to its users. They know what are regarded as masculine colours and designs, what is up-market and what is not. There is often more hearsay than science in their approach but at least the environment is considered. We are not aware of any such considerations being consciously acted on in the majority of British football clubs.

This is not to say that people's judgments on the relevance or influence of design are necessarily accurate. They may be very wide of the mark, but this will not influence how strongly they are held. More importantly it is often the case that beliefs influence what people do rather than any notionally 'objective' facts.

Taking these two principles of environmental psychology serves to show why the spectators' perspectives are so important. It is almost certain that their perspectives will differ from that of many other groups involved with football and that these differences will relate as much to symbolic or subjective aspects of football grounds and matches as to any overt observations.

It follows that the key to the future of professional football is in what *spectators* think about watching matches and what they think about the places in which it is played. It is these spectators who form views of the facilities, who feel welcome or not and who accept or create the patterns of activities associated with watching the game.

When you consider the importance of understanding the variety of viewpoints people hold; when you recognise the fact that supporters are likely to view a club very differently from its management; when you realise that the management itself is likely to think about the club differently from the way the police do, or the way in which Football Association officials do, then it is surprising how little attention has been paid to spectators' perspectives on football. It is assumed that because club directors watch a match and may once themselves have been spectators on the terraces that they implicitly understand what *all* groups of spectators want, even those groups from whom football clubs would plan to attract more paying customers in the future. Yet the problems of football discussed earlier suggest that club managements may not understand fully spectators' requirements or how to go about satisfying them.

DIFFERENCES BETWEEN CLUBS

The different perspectives do not develop in isolation. They are part of a set of interrelated factors including the environment and culture of which the person is a part. In effect, just as a group of plants and animals will develop into a balanced system, an ecology, so human groups form part of a system of interrelated perspectives. This can lead to important differences between different football clubs. As a consequence we need to understand the ways in which the whole atmosphere, or 'culture', of clubs may differ.

So far, we have considered football and football clubs as if they were one amorphous, homogeneous mass. Although they do have certain characteristics in common there are many differences between them. After all, British football clubs are named after the local community in which they grew up. For a long time players were actually drawn from that local community and aspiring professional footballers would only think of playing for their local, home team. As the game became more competitive the management of clubs became more overtly commercial so this local focus became less apparent. Players now may not even be nationals of the country in which they play.

Like market stalls and local concert halls that once were very much a showcase for the skills, crafts and talents of the local community, football clubs have now become part of a national and international market of footballing commodities. One can see the sponsoring of clubs by major international companies almost as part of the strange 'futures' market. They are investing in an anticipated future success which will give kudos to their firm by association. But the local context has not disappeared entirely. In some clubs it is more apparent than in others but all still have their own particular ethos. Associated with that are differences in attitudes and in the general behaviour of the club and its supporters.

It is important to recognise that these differences do exist because the experience of the facilities, the types of crowd behaviour that will occur and the management of a crowd will all take on different emphases in different locations. It is not only the size of the club or the division in which it is playing that creates the overall atmosphere of a football club, although both of these are important contributors, too. A set of expectations and rules of behaviour are all intertwined to give each club its own particular qualities.

These qualities may be a function of the history and environment in which the club operates or they may be a product of the supporters which the club has attracted over the years. Certainly just as those who play in the football teams are no longer drawn from the local community so the supporters are not necessarily local. Keen supporters will travel great distances to watch their favourite club. It is also worth noting that many supporters do, indeed, go to watch an interesting game of football rather than their own particular team. This means that spectators are not necessarily staunch supporters of a particular team, special to themselves. They may follow the fortunes of a number of clubs quite assiduously. The image of the two staunchly opposing sets of fans, as ritualistically antagonistic to each other as the players on the field, is a greatly oversimplified version of the actual complexities of interest and support that characterises spectators of a variety of different clubs. We have therefore devoted Chapter 4 to the consideration of club cultures.

CONTROL IS CRITICAL

A third point that emerges from the study of the impact of physical environments is that the stress they cause and the dissatisfaction they produce is often not a direct product of the quality of those surroundings. It is usually more directly related to the extent to which each person knows what is being demanded of him or her and the control they have over those demands. An intermittent noise that occurs at random and about which absolutely nothing can be done, is much more distracting than a constant, much louder noise that can be predicted and stopped if it gets too bothersome.

This notion of control is an important but complex one. Reason dictates that if you can choose where you go and what you do there, it is more likely that you will be satisfied with the actions and the place in which they happen. But for most of us, a lot of the time, this freedom is constrained both by the places available and what we are allowed to do there. So we keep some element of control by going to places where we know and accept what is allowed.

One way of thinking about this is that we like to be able to predict what is expected of us in any given place. Unpredictability causes anxiety. The more familiar a person is with a place the more predictable it is to them and so the more control, in a sense, they have over their actions there. Of course, there are big differences between people in the type of control they look for, but many people prefer a situation where they know what is expected of them and where they believe they are able to do what is expected.

This draws attention, then, to what some social scientists talk of as the 'rule-system' in any situation. An amusing, rather unusual, example serves to illustrate how we can take complex rules for granted, forgetting they exist. We once took a Cameroonian friend to a Christmas pantomime. She was enthralled by the glitter and spectacle she had never seen before, but she was particularly impressed by the audience response to the people on stage and the precision and vehemence with which the audience responded, as one, to the now traditional jibes from the actors. After the performance, our visitor asked in all seriousness if the people in the audience had rehearsed their responses. She could not see how else they could have performed in such unison. If we had visited her country we might have felt the same way about the responses given in church by the congregation, wondering in our turn about how the audience knew what to say when.

Gospel chants or pantomime shouts are just extreme examples of what happens daily in many other ways. We are educated into modes of behaving and responding in many different situations. What environmental psychologists are beginning to uncover is that these rule-systems are characteristic of certain places as well as of certain activities.

One of the most important consequences of all the above processes is what has been called the self-fulfilling prophecy. This is the process whereby we all expect certain people to be, and particular activities to occur, in particular locations. We then decide whether we wish to be part of those events. If we do, we go to that place and take part, or indeed initiate what we consider to be appropriate activity. By our actions we fulfil the prophecy we ourselves have made.

This mechanism can be readily illustrated from many common situations. Say, for instance, you believe a party will be a riotous affair with people cavorting in some degree of wild abandon. If you do not want to be part of such an event you will stay away. Provided a number of others share your view of the likely party and decide they wish to enjoy such an event, they will turn up in an appropriate mood (and with the appropriate spirit no doubt). This is then likely to produce the lively party you feared. Because of the prophecy, people made the action occur. If the prophecy had not been made it would be less likely to occur. So, the prophecy fulfilled itself.

The problem with some of these processes is that they are difficult to break. If football matches are seen as places to go and shout and yell at, then those who like shouting and yelling will go. It would take a very concerted effort to attract very different people with very different expectations before this could be reversed.

As will become apparent in more detail in later chapters, the messages, rules and self-fulfilling prophecies all have great significance in the understanding of many aspects of football grounds and the activities associated with them. They help to show why small-scale piecemeal attempts to deal with these problems are doomed to failure.

Crowd Management and Emergencies

A further aspect of the theme of personal control in thinking about football and football grounds is the fact that large numbers of people in these very special types of settings pose a particular problem of management and organisation. This is a problem that takes on more dramatic proportions when there is an emergency. Of course, part of the essence of crowd management and control is to make sure that an emergency does not happen; but as we have seen over the past twenty years a number of emergencies continues to occur in and around football games. This is partly a function of the size and number of people involved and the fact that they are brought together in a constrained space with limited access and limited possibilities for leaving.

We tend tacitly to assume that thousands of people can leave a large space through a limited number of corridors and exit doors. Yet even the simplest calculation will reveal that it would be very easy for the crowd to become jammed in a limited escape route. Traffic jams in cities are just a large scale version of the problems that can happen with pedestrians. The problem is compounded by the fact that people will typically wish to arrive over an extended period of time but will all wish to leave at once. In an emergency they would wish to leave in some hurry.

The emergencies that can occur are not limited to the obvious disasters that can be caused by rapid crowd movements, running from fires and fights. Bomb scares are not unknown in football grounds and the collapse of the physical fabric itself does, of course, give rise to very dangerous situations.

What emerges from an examination of crowd management is that the processes of communication between the people responsible for that management and the communication to the crowd as a whole, is absolutely critical to safe evacuation under normal circumstances. It is this communication that is often the difference between life and death in emergency situations. This is rather different from the popular myth that any dangerous event such as fire or some other emergency will inevitably give rise to uncontrolled flight and wild, mindless panic.

The problem of crowd control therefore becomes one of having carefully prepared plans and good effective communications that are ready for possible emergency. This turns out to be more difficult than might first seem to be the case. A large number of people leaving a stadium does not behave like a flow of water passing through a pipe. People will choose one route in preference to another, they will wait or look for friends. People do not necessarily fill the whole available exit channel in the manner of a liquid, nor do they all start to move together in one even action.

All these differences from the flow of inanimate material pose especial difficulties for calculating how quickly people will leave a large building when under some life-endangering threat. The problem is magnified by the knowledge and expectations that we had cause to mention earlier in relation to other aspects of watching football. This means that simply calculating the speed at which people walk and then putting it into some general estimates of numbers and exit widths is unlikely to give very accurate answers. A more systematic study of human behaviour is required. The results of such studies are reviewed in Chapter 4.

CROWD AGGRESSION AND VIOLENCE

One of the main dilemmas of present-day British football, central to our book, is that the excitement and enjoyment associated with being part of a large, lively crowd can also be felt as threatening. In many people's minds hooliganism and football are closely intertwined. Without doubt it is one, but not the only, important contribution to people staying away from football matches. A number of surveys has shown the significance of this fear. In the *British Crime Survey* of 1984, 10 per cent of men said that the threat of violence kept them away. A year or so later our own *Survey of Supporters*, to be reported in more detail in later chapters, revealed that 20 per cent of respondents would be encouraged to go to football matches more often if violence was reduced. In a MORI public opinion survey of 2,069 people in the summer of 1985, 25 per cent of people gave potential violence as a reason for not going to football matches. This compared with 17 per cent who said they preferred to watch football on television.

This association in the popular imagination is interesting in its own right. Why should people immediately think of football hooliganism but not of cricket hooliganism or horse racing hooliganism? The ready answer is the frequency of its occurrence, but this is not supported by close examination.

For example, many of the acts that are described as football hooliganism do not take place within football grounds and are only very loosely associated with people going to football matches. Furthermore, acts of violence or vandalism that do not occur in association with football are more likely to be described as the criminal acts they are rather than obtain headlines under the label of 'hooliganism'. So the sets of expectations that journalists and other people have about football help to generate greater awareness of things that happen that may support those expectations. This self-fulfilling prophecy then intertwines with the other expectations discussed earlier.

When a close look is taken at actual incidents that have been labelled as 'hooligan' then a great variety of actions is apparent. At its most benign level it is gangs of young men shouting abuse at each other. At its most vicious it is an extended battle in which blood is drawn and lives are lost. By looking closely at the offences that people in football crowds have been charged with, Eugene Trivizas[3] has shown that offenders are rarely charged with criminal damage or assault. The most common charge was for threatening or insulting behaviour, accounting for 438 offences out of the 652 examined, just over two-thirds. Only two cases were for assault.

The other myth that Trivizas scotches is that the offenders are all working-class youths. Only 1 in 5 was under 17 years old. Two-thirds were aged between 17 and 20 and the remainder were older. These 'hooligans' are certainly not schoolboys. The indications are that the people arrested were typically manual workers, far more of them being employed than unemployed.

Not a lot is understood about the circumstances under which the typical, abusive behaviour changes into the much rarer violence or vandalism. There is not even clear evidence that the two extremes of aggression are closely connected. What evidence there is, though, will be discussed in Chapter 6. This indicates that some of the dangerous and damaging activities that occur in association with football do grow out of much less dangerous and less intentionally malicious activities. But there is also evidence that some components of football violence are part of a very malicious, planned activity.

There is also clear evidence to show that the courts do not deal with acts of violence associated with football in the same way as they do when it is associated with other activities. The work of Eugene Trivizas has already been mentioned. He is a lecturer in Criminology and Penology at the University of Reading. He has carried out a number of studies of the legal aspects of football hooliganism, and from a detailed study of sentencing of offenders he concludes that:

> Persons committing offences in football crowd disorders were punished more severely than persons committing similar offences in other circumstances.[4]

On average, Trivizas shows, football related offenders are fined about half as much again as those charged with the same crime in circumstances unrelated to a football match. Whatever the reason, the courts see acts of aggression committed within the context of football crowds as more serious than similar acts in crowds of demonstrators or other incidents.

There are many reasons why there is a variety of legal differences in the way anti-social acts associated with football are treated when compared with similar acts in other contexts. For example, the size of a football crowd may be such that policemen may need to be drawn in from a variety of distant locations in order to police a match. Policemen are men and women, often with spouses and families. Any arrests and charges they make that will be contested may require them to return at some distance to take part in local court proceedings. They would not be human if they did not sometimes try to avoid such inconvenience. Furthermore, the charges that are brought will often be charges that it is known will bring convictions with the type of evidence available in a large crowd disturbance. This may mean that many actions that could more appropriately be placed under one heading, but which would demand stronger evidence, will be placed under a different heading with more hope of achieving a conviction. These and other similar matters make the close examination of the legal proceedings surrounding football violence very problematic.

A further complication comes from the perspectives that are held on football and the aggression associated with it. Clearly there is some feeling that there is a particularly disturbing quality to acts of aggression that occur in large crowds brought together to support the symbolic conflict between two opposing teams. There is not a great deal of detailed study but the fact that football is banned as a professional game on Sundays goes back to the puritanical view that playing football is not a particularly wholesome activity and too frivolous to watch on the Lord's day. The argument has not been expressed as such for many years but is easy to find below the surface, in cartoons and other examples, that going to watch a football match is a direct dereliction of domestic and other duties. Such a view provides a breeding ground within which unfavourable views can easily be born and reproduced. However, these attitudes towards the potential unsavouriness of football crowds and the football-watching activity do not really go very far towards explaining why violence has been associated with football spectators so consistently during the course of this century.

In recent years there has been a number of attempts to understand football violence and hooliganism more directly. The explanations that have emerged from these studies have usually been one of three kinds. One explanation has drawn on ideas about the nature of people and the animal origins of aggressive behaviour between groups. A second has related to the nature of the activity itself and the ways in which it stimulates or generates particular types of aggressive action. A third type of explanation has been a broad social one seeing football violence as a reflection of wider problems of aggression and violence within society as a whole. Each of these explanations has some germ of truth within it and we shall try to put together our view of their combined perspective in Chapter 5.

In focusing on the association of hooliganism and football and explanations for it, it is easy to be driven to the situation where it is difficult to understand why violence does not normally occur at football matches. For that is certainly the truth of the matter. Hooliganism and violence associated with football matches takes up a very small proportion of the total range of crowd activities involved. Good humour and moderately impolite badinage is far more the hallmark of a football crowd than is any act of aggression. Considering the millions of people who go to watch football in Britain each Saturday, the few thousand who are arrested for threatening or insulting behaviour during the course of a football year account for a very small portion. On average there are less than 5 arrests per 10,000 spectators, although a few large incidents will distort this average greatly. It follows, as a consequence, that any explanation of football hooliganism must take account of why it does not usually occur and provide an understanding of the particular circumstances in which it is likely to occur.

The explanation of hooliganism and football-related violence is not a purely academic matter. It is central to any sensible attempt to control it. If the problem is one of particular types of people or of particular innate characteristics of individuals, then approaches to control would need to keep such people out of football grounds. If, on the other hand, the problem was a product of the particular circumstances themselves, the place, the culture, the perspectives, then these would need to be managed and controlled more effectively. Explanation and its implications for approaches to controlling football hooliganism, then, are a central feature of later chapters. But it must be emphasised that this is such a central feature because of the public awareness of the association of hooliganism with football and its direct implications on whether football supporters will be prepared to attend football matches. It is this interplay of attitude, explanation and approaches to control that makes the whole issue so much more complex than might be apparent from the headlines in popular newspapers.

The violence that breaks out from time to time at large sporting events is a product of who goes to those events, where they take place and what happens at them. As we have indicated there is an identifiable, if subtle, interplay between people, place and activities.

FOOTBALL IN ITS PLACE

This interplay is shaped by the expectations, attitudes and perspectives that people have. It will take different forms in different cultural contexts and it will be modified by the processes of crowd management and control. We are concerned to elaborate the details of this complex system both as a way of illustrating the nature and contribution of environmental psychology and as a way of helping football and other spectator sports find their place.

THE WAY FORWARD

As we have seen, football is a special combination of particular circumstances. It has a problem that relates to those circumstances and to the particular place football plays in our national consciousness. Major public inquiries throughout the century have made recommendations in relation to improving football but still various problems continue and, virtually as a consequence, the resources available for solving them are reduced. Against this background there cannot be any simple, straightforward single answer to football's predicament. Yet the answer to falling attendances and a bad press does lie with the football clubs themselves.

What other area of public recreation exists that has seen a 60 per cent drop in support over forty years? Is there any other activity, once paramount, that has seen such competition for the recreational pound from other more family-orientated recreational and leisure attractions? Is there another large spectator activity where the physical conditions in which clients partake of the recreation have not improved much over fifty years, so that a majority of the paying customers is expected to stand on cold, wind and rain-swept expanses of concrete terracing for two hours or more with less than basic lavatory and refreshment facilities? Is there any other area of public entertainment for which, over the last five years, nearly 100 spectators died, either through the irresponsible and aggressive activities of a small section of the client group, or deficiencies in the design and management of the physical facilities of the spectator attraction?

It is not surprising to find any such a recreational activity in chronic financial difficulties. Yet for most others you would assume that their management would be desperately trying to impose a range of solutions to reverse their fortunes and attract back the clients they have lost. Or you might expect it to be a minority interest that is being allowed to die slowly. Yet this is no bizarre and curious little-known sport. It's professional football in Great Britain.

Yet football is still an enormously popular spectator sport. The World Cup final can attract a world-wide television audience of 500 million viewers. In Britain ordinary League matches televised on Sunday afternoons are viewed by several million people. Millions of pounds of sponsorship are injected into football each year. Such sponsorship goes not only to the glamour clubs but also to those in the lower divisions and even non Football League teams. To be a footballer is still a dream of many children, and like some other sports and pop music, it offers a ticket 'out of the ghetto'. Football, then, is still the number one spectator sport in Britain. Football therefore does, at present, have tremendous resources and goodwill on which to draw but, if the current decline in attendances continues and football managements remain so unadventurous in their approach to their paying clients, it could be a minority sport in Great Britain before the twentieth century draws to a close.

The former manager of Liverpool Football Club, the late Bill Shankley, once said, 'Some people think football is as important as life and death. I can assure them that it is much more serious than that.' Indeed, as soon as normally sane and rational people start discussing football, reason and balanced judgment can fly out of the window. Standards and criteria which are applied to other places, activities and organisations are all too often forgotten. Football inhabits a world of its own as a recreational activity and spectator sport. The terms and conditions of some of its ˙mployees are arguably as over-generous as the facilities and conditions which the paying customer has to endure are mean. We believe that this is one of the fundamental problems of football today. It is our view that football should be assessed like any other recreational activity for the public, in which the football spectator is seen as an important client whose attention, interest, comfort and support should constantly be sought, encouraged and maintained. If football grounds were construed by football clubs as visitor attractions in competition with the best visitor and tourist attractions, quite different standards of facilities and services would be expected and required.

Here, then, is the key to the solutions to the complex problems of football. Certainly professional football is an integrated and significant part of our society. It does not exist in isolation. The social, legal and communal environment in which it exists provides important constraints and opportunities that shape its nature. But beyond all this it is a mass entertainment of potential attraction to a wide variety of people. By embracing this basic notion many changes will follow.

For example, the reader will have noticed that we have referred to the supporter as 'he', thereby making the same assumption that football clubs make – that is, the football supporter is male. However, the proportion of women attending football matches is not insignificant. In a MORI poll conducted in 1985, in which a random sample of 2,069 people were asked how often they go to watch a football match at a League club, 4 per cent of women interviewed said they attended a match at least once a year, compared with 20 per cent of men. If this is an accurate reflection of the proportion of males and females who attend football matches, this would suggest that on average up to one-fifth of the people attending a Football League match are women. This ties in with the 1983 *General Household Survey*, which suggests that 1 person in 6 attending a Football League match is female. Yet the facilities for women are quite simply appalling at most football grounds.

Consider also the continuing debates about the ownership of grounds. These rarely relate to the spectators' experience. They are almost always seen in pure profit terms. For example, Charlton Athletic have had to leave The Valley, because the owners of the ground acquired planning permission to build a supermarket on the site and so the site value increased considerably. Charlton Athletic now share a ground with Crystal Palace at Selhurst Park. Bristol Rovers play on the ground of Southern League team, Bath City, in the neighbouring town! For the spectator this means high travelling costs and disenchantment. Such moves might be more understandable and acceptable if they led to improvements in the facilities and services for supporters. It is doubtful whether this is ever the case, or whether this has even been considered.

The scale of the resources football clubs have is apparent as you fly over any city. There is always one major aspect of the urban architecture that stands out, because of its size and the dominant form it has in the city landscape. This is the sports stadium. Outside of the baseball belt of North America, these stadia are invariably oval or rectangular because their primary purpose is to house spectators watching professional football. Yet, curiously, as dominant as these places are from the air, they do not play a very large part in our discussions of the city and its facilities. Attention is drawn to football grounds when there are acts of crowd violence associated with them, when there are major fires, or other headline-catching disasters there. As a consequence of this sporadic silence about football grounds, there is now a real risk that these potentially enormous community resources will lose their function because their original, primary objective for being there – football matches – are losing their public attraction. Football has an identifiable place, physically in the urban fabric and spiritually (or symbolically), in our ideas about society. The football authorities must recognise this significance and respond to it positively if football is to maintain its place.

Chapter Two

SPECTATORS' VIEWS

Experts on the Terraces

In most situations and with most problem areas trust is placed in the opinion of experts. To take two obvious examples, we may go to a doctor with our health problems or to an estate agent to sell a house. Public or private inquiries and the courts may call on experts or expert witnesses to give their opinion of the issues in question. Our trust in these experts is based on two things – their training in a certain field such as medicine, civil engineering or stadium management, and their experience of working in that field. A new practitioner fresh from a training course is not yet considered expert. Real expertise comes from repeated experience.

Often it seems that only professionals are considered to be experts, that formal qualifications, letters after the name, are what counts. As environmental psychologists we take a different view, however, putting forward the case for the user (or consumer) as expert. This view relies more heavily on the second facet of expertise – experience – and suggests that many of the real experts on the subject of watching football are the spectators. The emphasis is placed not on one opinion from an outsider but on a number of opinions covering the broad experience of football. This is not to deny the value of outside judgments. It is often profitable, for instance, to study emergencies at football matches and the behaviour of those involved, from the point of view of an outsider. This throws into relief a series of highly-charged dramatic and extreme incidents. The real story of football, however, is about events in a popular, normal, weekly event, in many ways a routine occurrence, albeit often surrounded with non-routine excitement.

In order to find out more about this event, therefore, we asked some experts – nearly 1,000 football supporters - for their perspective on football. What did they think about the facilities at football grounds? Were they reasonably comfortable during matches? Did they feel safe from violence or accident? Where in the ground was safest? How racist was the crowd and did political groups provoke violence at their ground? We were also interested in lapsed supporters: those who had been regular visitors to the ground until a year or two ago, but who had now stopped attending. We wanted to discover who these people were, why they withdrew their support and whether their views differed from those of current supporters.

What psychology brings to this survey of views and opinions is a methodology which enables us to draw inferences about the views of football spectators as a group from the views of many individuals. It is not always possible to summarise the views of a group of people without discounting important differences within them. In this case we have looked for differences between supporters depending on whether they are current or lapsed, which club they support and even whether they prefer to sit or to stand. The differences we are interested in are not simply differences in the number of people who agree with any statement, but rather the underlying difference in attitude which that discrepancy may represent. Therefore, rather than place weight on single questions we look at trends across a number of issues so as to have a broader understanding of the spectator's perspective.

Ten clubs were chosen to give a range across size, wealth, League position and location. They were Celtic, Coventry City, Chelsea, Fulham, Manchester United, Millwall, Preston North End, Southampton, Sunderland and Tottenham Hotspur. As the survey was carried out in 1985, all the comments refer to that time. Although we asked all ten clubs if they had made any changes since then, only three, Manchester United, Millwall and Sunderland, replied to this question. These clubs had made some interesting improvements, in crowd control measures, in trying to attract more families and in community involvement.

Once the clubs had been chosen, interviewers found local supporters by calling on houses near the ground. The sample therefore represents the views of people supporting their local team, rather than those ardent supporters who may follow a team hundreds of miles from where they live. A comparison of our respondents with those who took part in other surveys suggests that they are representative of football supporters generally.[1]

We were interested in two types of supporters: those who attended matches regularly at the time of the interview and those who had given up within the last two years. These two groups are referred to from now on as 'regular' and as 'lapsed' respectively. In the case of each club, half those interviewed were selected to be regular and half lapsed, so that we could compare the views of these two groups and look at the reasons people gave for their lapsed support. The respondents were selected to be roughly half over 25 years old and half under, so there would be a balance of views from younger and more mature supporters.

One advantage of carrying out the interviews in the respondents' homes rather than at matches was that more time could be allowed for the interview and so more open-ended questions could be asked than is normally possible. This allowed us to ask supporters how they would improve the ground without making suggestions which might influence them in any way. It released us from the constraint of having to ask people to choose from a list of what we thought the alternatives were, rather than getting their opinion directly.

Four main topics were covered in the interview: (a) comfort and conditions, (b) possible improvements, (c) reasons for no longer attending matches and (d) spectator violence.

Comfort and conditions covered such topics as the physical conditions at the ground and how comfortable it was, either standing or sitting. Respondents were also asked what improvements they thought the club should make and which of these improvements was a priority. One specific improvement we asked about was the introduction of more seating. We dealt with this specifically because all-seater stadia have often been discussed in government reports as an important way forward for football.

We asked lapsed supporters why they had stopped going to football matches and what they thought might attract more people to matches. We also looked at the differences between the views of lapsed and regular supporters on the other issues to see whether those who had lapsed were more dissatisfied with the levels of comfort and safety.

We asked people what they thought about violence at soccer matches, whether they had ever been worried about their safety, whether they thought political groups might be involved in provoking violence and what they thought of the police presence in and around the grounds. We also explored their attitudes to what might be called violence-related issues, such as racist language and 'mickey-taking'.

One important component of the experience of a ground is the size of crowd it normally attracts. If the ground normally operates near full capacity then there may be crowding. Queues and facilities, such as toilets and refreshment stands, will be stretched to the limit. On the positive side, the atmosphere will be more exciting and the club should be doing well financially. If a ground is often quite empty, there is less stress on facilities and space but the atmosphere may be dull, bad weather more noticeable and the club may be heading for financial difficulties. In any case, the size of the gate reflects the fortunes of the club and it would be strange indeed if this did not colour the experience of 'being there'. We have therefore listed clubs in subsequent figures in order of their average gate taken as a proportion of their ground's capacity, Celtic being the most consistently full ground and Coventry the least.

THE SUPPORTERS

The football supporters who took part in this survey tended to be young, even though the sample was selected to split respondents evenly between under and over 25 years old. Three-quarters of them were under 30 and nearly a third were under 20. This reflects the composition of football crowds and is similar to the age distribution found in other studies.

Most were what is usually called working class, i.e. skilled and unskilled manual workers, although there was also a sizeable percentage of white-collar workers. The socioeconomic characteristics of the respondents must depend to some extent on the character of the area around each stadium, because of the way the sample was selected. However, as a bias towards the working class is usually found in studies of football spectators, we can assume that the sample of men who took part in the survey is representative of male football supporters in general.

Our respondents tended to be quite committed as supporters. Even those who had now stopped going to football were keen in their day. About three-quarters of respondents described themselves as regular supporters (Fig. 2.1) and half went to all or nearly all of their clubs' home matches, with a further 20 per cent going once a month (Fig. 2.2). Just under half the respondents also travelled to watch their team play away matches (Fig. 2.3). Their interest in football was generally confined to their local club. Nearly three-quarters only went to see their own team play, although this proportion varied across clubs and depended on whether there was more than one club in that particular area. In London, where a number of clubs are close together, people were more likely to watch other teams as well as the one they lived closest to.

In summary, in keeping with other samples of football supporters, we found that the men who took part in the survey were mostly young and working class and were committed to supporting their home team, and even those who had now lapsed had been reasonably regular attenders when they did go to matches.

Comfort and conditions

Over two-thirds of respondents thought that their ground was comfortable or quite comfortable. In addition, almost all respondents thought that the conditions at their ground were average or above. On the other hand, only just over one-third thought that their ground was alright as it is, needing no improvement. Sixty-four per cent thought that improvements would encourage more people to go to matches. Twenty-eight per cent said that they themselves would go more often. Two reasons were given for not going even in improved conditions: either they felt that they already attended as often as possible, or they had given up watching football matches altogether and could not be tempted back. The improvements suggested ranged from basic upgrading of the facilities offered to more substantial changes aimed at encouraging more people and certain groups in particular to come to football matches. On the basic level respondents wanted the ground to be clean, structurally sound and to have adequate, clean toilets.

What Would You Improve?

'All of it. It's pretty dirty and very basic.'

Celtic

'The first thing is the toilet facilities, they're the worst in the Football League.'

Millwall

Figure 2.1 Percentage of yes and no answers to the question: "Do/did you go regularly to the ground?"

Figure 2.2 Percentage responses to the question: "How often do/did you go to the ground?"

Figure 2.3 Percentage who watched their team last season.

A typical example of a structural improvement is to provide some sort of weatherproofing.

> 'I think they should have a roof-covering for the supporters. You can't expect people to pay £3 [1985 prices] to stand in the rain.'
>
> Fulham

This quote is also an example of many respondents feeling that the conditions they encountered at football grounds were simply not of a high enough standard for the sort of money they were paying for tickets. Another set of suggested improvements concerned things such as family enclosures or increasing the number of seats.

> 'Have a family enclosure and try to entice the right people to the game.'
>
> Fulham

Many of these suggestions are aimed at encouraging 'respectable' supporters and families back to football as a way to combat football hooliganism, a theme to which we shall return in the final chapter.

Fifty-seven per cent thought that making the ground all seated would improve attendance, but again mostly that of 'other people'. Whether these 'other people' exist is a moot point but the tone suggests that supporters feel improvements would be useful and make the game more attractive. These supporters may feel that, while they themselves are keen enough to put up with discomfort for the sake of the team, for other less enthusiastic supporters the disadvantages may outweigh the advantages.

The supporter's perception of the views held by generalised 'others' is an important illustration of a phenomenon well recognised by social scientists. It reflects people's ideas of the 'image' they see football as having; the way it is thought of or perceived by people in general. This has many ramifications for the future of football, the support it will get from the public at large and those who see themselves as representing that public. But it also means that supporters are unlikely to try and convince their friends and associates to come to matches because the supporter expects a rebuff, in part because of existing conditions.

SPECTATORS' VIEWS

WHY PEOPLE NO LONGER GO TO FOOTBALL MATCHES

Much concern has been expressed, both in this volume and elsewhere, about the number of people now attending football matches. Indeed, of the ten clubs in this survey, eight had a drop in attendances between 1984–5 and 1985–6. We felt that it was important to look at the reasons for this drop in attendance in some detail. We took two approaches to the problem. First, we asked people for their reasons for not going to matches anymore. Second, we compared lapsed with present supporters to see whether certain types of supporter were more likely to lapse.

The threat of violence at or near football grounds is probably the most often cited reason for the fall in attendances. The feeling is that 'real' fans and families are too frightened to go to matches any more, not wanting to risk being caught up in any disruptions. It can be argued that if people who fear violence are less likely to go, the proportion of the crowd for whom it is not a threat will tend to increase. This increase can then provide the context within which disruptive or anti-social behaviour can increase. This is a self-fulfilling prophecy. Once football grounds are labelled as violent places that very label ensures that they will get even more violent.

Indeed, when we looked at the reasons lapsed supporters gave for quitting, violence and safety were mentioned by more people than any other factors. However, while violence stands out if we look at the reasons one by one, it is eclipsed by the total number of other, more mundane reasons given. Losing interest in football was mentioned 69 times with people saying, for example, that they had grown out of the pastime. The poor performance of the local team came up 72 times, with supporters giving up if the club had a run of failure or dropped to a lower division in the League. Respondents also blamed other commitments, such as working or playing football themselves. Others could no longer afford the admission charges, thought it too uncomfortable or inconvenient, or had simply moved away from the vicinity of the ground and did not want to make the extra effort that attending would now involve.

Although worry about violence and safety is therefore undoubtedly keeping people away from football, this is only one of a number of disincentives. In other words, many of these lapsed supporters would not be won back simply by hooligan-free stadia. They want to watch a successful team play exciting football and are not likely to stick with their home team through thick and thin.

One way to look at what sorts of supporters give up football as a pastime is to compare how solid their support was when they did go with the regularity of the support of current supporters. In the great majority of cases the regular supporters go to matches more often than the lapsed supporters ever did (Fig. 2.4). This is a finding supported by market research and well in accord with common sense. It is the fan(atic) who sticks with a club through thick and thin and the occasional supporter who is most likely to lose interest if the game is less attractive for any reason.

Lapsed supporters are less likely to see the home ground as a special preserve (Fig. 2.5). They are also more concerned to enjoy watching the game than simply to see their team win (Fig. 2.6).

These differences might be thought of as differences in lapsed supporters' overall approach to the game, i.e. they may place more emphasis on certain aspects such as entertainment value. One comparison illuminates this further. We presented people with the statement, 'It's alright to take the mickey out of the other side's football supporters.' It is difficult to ask people questions about attitudes which they know are socially unacceptable because they are likely to give you the answer they believe to be the acceptable one. Therefore, instead of asking for views on hooliganism, we asked about attitudes toward a mild degree of confrontation, using the slightly more acceptable term 'mickey-taking', in the hope that this would give some clues about attitudes towards more serious manifestations of inter-club rivalry. We are not suggesting that all those who think that mickey-taking is acceptable are hooligans. However, these people are more likely to be tolerant of physical aggression than are those who do not even tolerate taunts. Of particular interest in the responses were the big variations between clubs. For Sunderland even such a mild statement is only acceptable to 16 per cent, but for Celtic regulars and Manchester United supporters it is endorsed by over 60 per cent (Fig. 2.7). These club differences will be considered in more detail in Chapter 3, but for the present they serve to illustrate the discriminatory power of this and related attitudinal questions.

From the point of view of the general argument the trend towards the regulars being more prepared to accept 'mickey-taking' and the lapsed less so is an important piece of the jigsaw. The trend is small

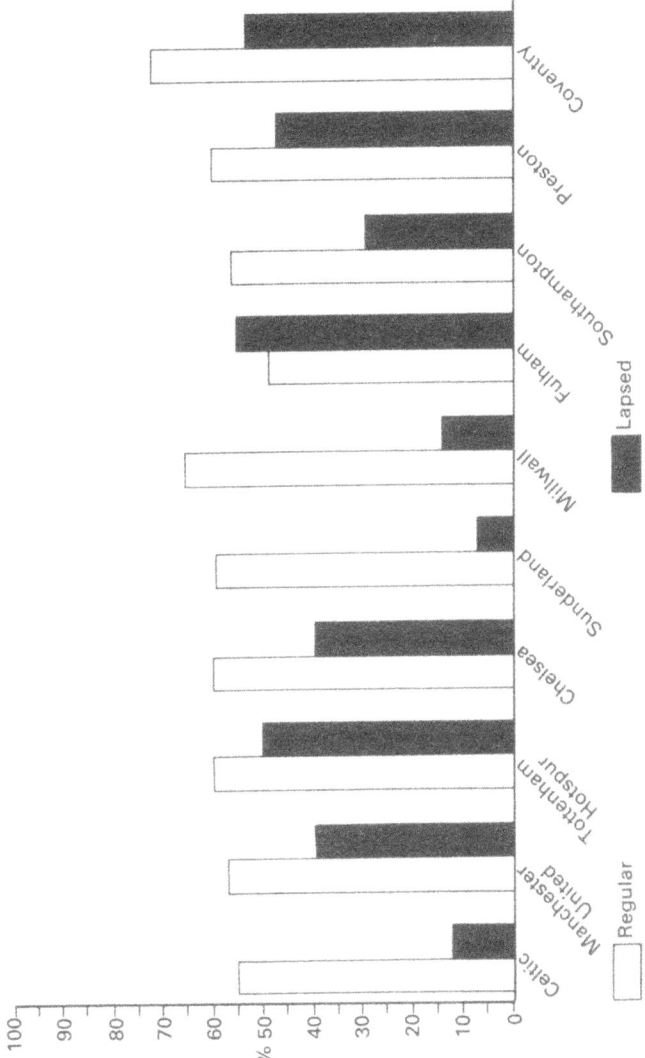

Figure 2.4 Comparison of the percentage of lapsed and regular supporters who said they went to most games, at each of ten clubs.

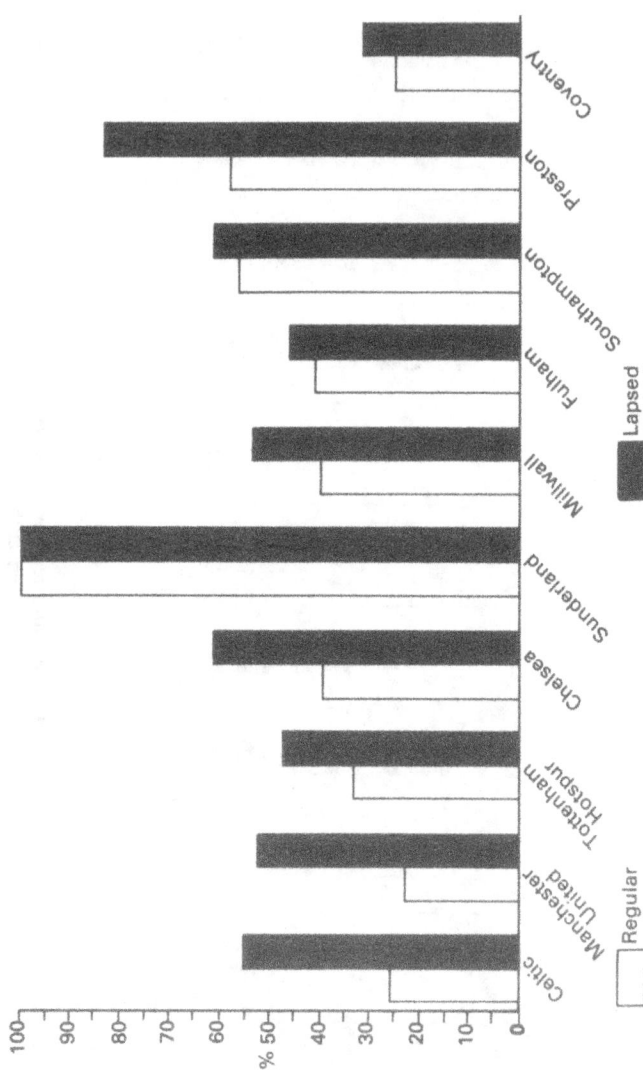

Figure 2.5 Comparison of the percentage of lapsed and regular supporters who said it was all right to share the home ground, at each of ten clubs.

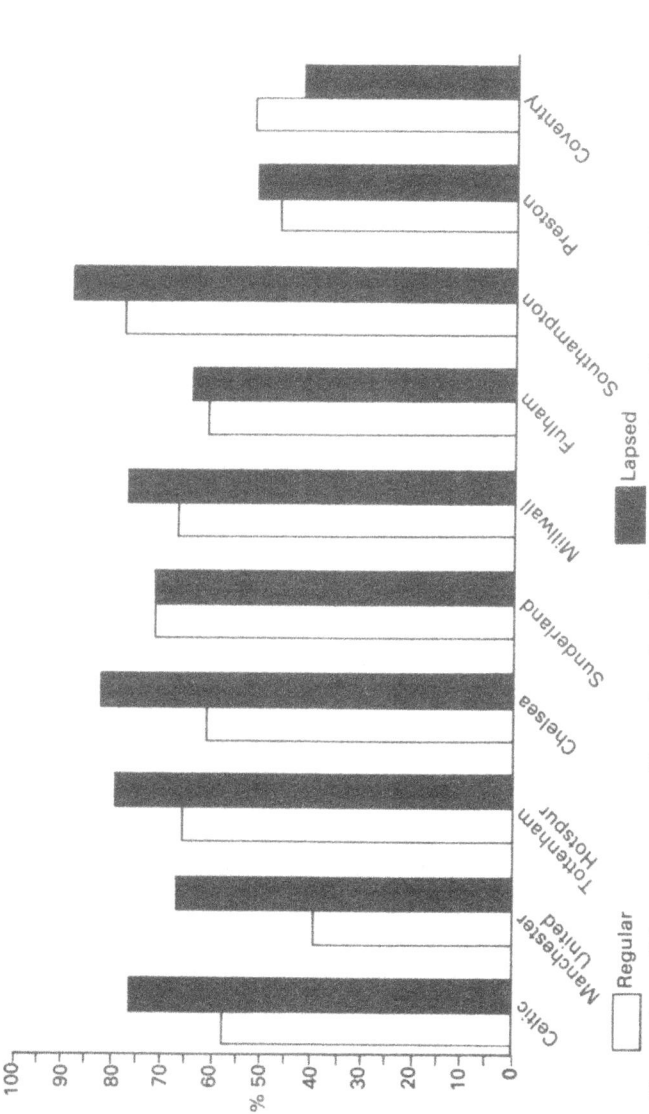

Figure 2.6 Comparison of the percentage of lapsed and regular supporters who said an enjoyable game was more important than winning, at each of ten clubs.

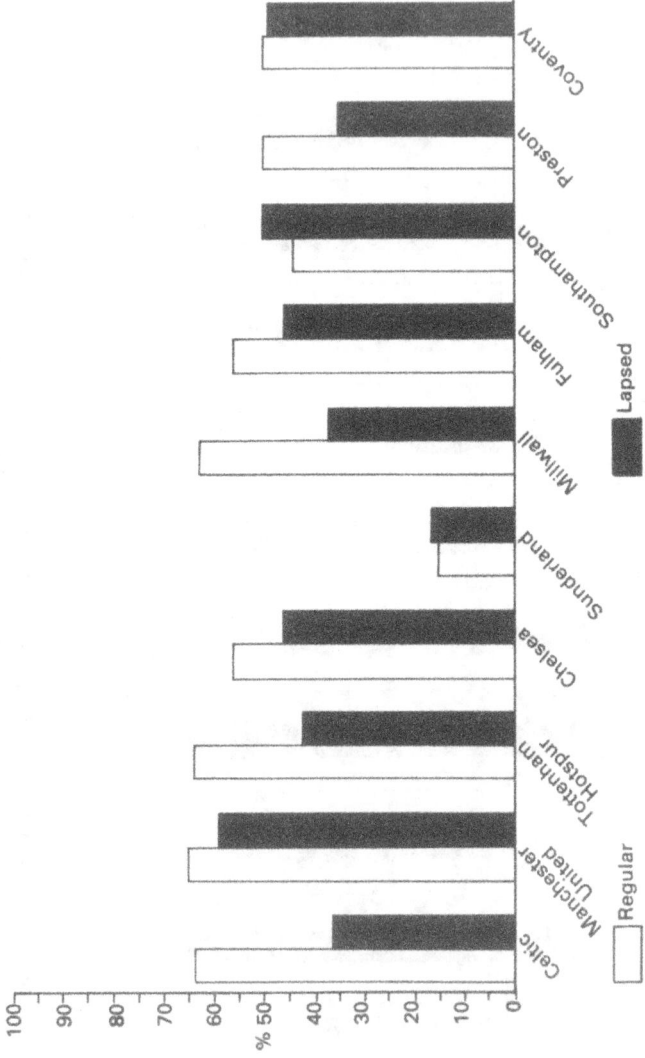

Figure 2.7 Comparison of the percentage of lapsed and regular supporters who said "it's all right to take the mickey", at each of ten clubs.

but overall those who accept the statement are in the majority in the regular group and in the minority amongst the lapsed.

It would be wrong to place too much credence on these small but consistent differences taken on their own. They do, however, reveal a tendency that accords with two other sources of data. First, as we have mentioned already, there has been a fall-off in the numbers attending football since the Second World War. The decline has not been constant but the overall trend is downwards. Second, there has been an upward trend in the number of arrests relative to attendance for clubs in the London area. Therefore, while attendances drop, arrests increase. The patterns of data we are talking about show only small subtle differences but until we have full clear records of all incidents of crowd disorders and until we know more about how small outbreaks of abuse and scuffles relate to near riots it would be foolish to dismiss the consistencies indicated here.

The critical point here is that the overall decline in attendances appears to relate to a process that might be likened to distillation. It is the ardent fans who are most likely to remain faithful to the club. These supporters are also likely to be more tolerant of aggression. The 'real' supporters are not, in fact, being scared off by hooligans. It is the occasional enthusiasts who have withdrawn their support. This is grim news for the club management, who must attract back to football not the traditional supporter but the more fickle and less easily pleased crowds who can fill the stadium on the right occasions.

Safety

Because worry about safety was so important, being the initial reason for the survey, we explored the issue in further detail. One question asked was, 'Have you ever been worried for your safety when you have been going to, leaving, or at a match?' The question was deliberately directed at people's worries about themselves, rather than at their witnessing of events where the safety of others may have been endangered, or at general opinions of how safe football grounds are. We wanted to know of direct experiences rather than of hearsay or public images. Looking at the number of people who answered yes, it is hard to believe that the event in question is supposed to be entertainment. Over one-third of the respondents had been worried at some time (Fig. 2.8). For Coventry this figure goes up to almost two-thirds. In fact, for all clubs except Sunderland more than 1 person in 4 had worried about their safety. The low percentage at Sunderland is interesting. If all the clubs had had more or less the same number of supporters who answered yes to this question then we might conclude that the worry was simply linked to going to football matches. A small proportion of any large crowd may be anxious, whether it be because they are nervous people or because the experience of being part of a large crowd may be inherently frightening. Because of the wide variation in the number of worried people across clubs we can reasonably conclude that the worry is caused by spectators at some clubs having been exposed to dangerous situations of one sort or another.

To examine this issue further, we asked people to recount what had happened at the time they were worried. The incidents fell into three categories: (a) violence caused by fans, (b) crushing caused by crowding and (c) crushing caused by mounted police. Which category was mentioned most often varied from club to club but the most commonly reported type was violence caused by fans. We looked in more detail at the five clubs which had the highest percentage of worried supporters.

Violence caused by fans

Although respondents were not asked about the previous season in particular, it is worth pointing out that Coventry City had had its fair share of crowd trouble in the season before the survey was carried out. During the 1984–5 season there were pitch invasions on 1 September at the match against Leicester and again on 29 September, when the opposing side was Arsenal. On 1 January Manchester City fans rioted, ripping out around 500 seats. Therefore there had been ample opportunity that season for Coventry City fans to witness crowd trouble at first hand. The other clubs did not have entirely quiet seasons either. Celtic had trouble on 7 November during their match against Rapid Vienna, which was serious enough for a UEFA ruling that the match should be replayed at least 100 miles from Glasgow. Crowd violence at Chelsea in a match against Southampton on 20 October led to Chelsea fans being banned from visiting Southampton. Chelsea had more trouble

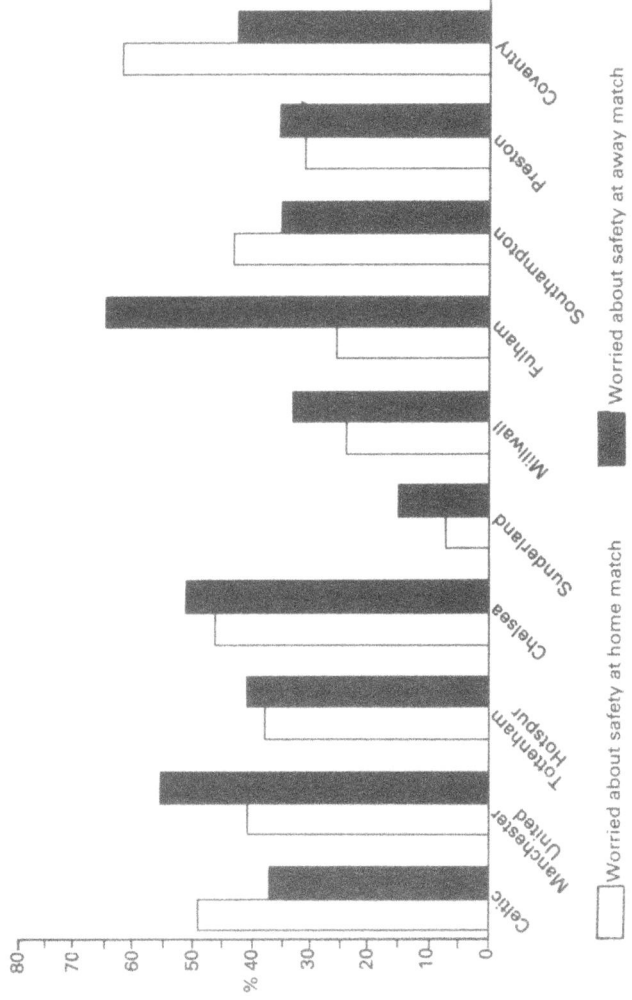

Figure 2.8 Comparisons of the proportions worried about safety at home and away matches, at each of ten clubs.

on 4 March when mounted police were called in to deal with a pitch invasion during the Sunderland match.

These are the major incidents that occurred at these grounds. They take no account of minor scuffles or of recurrent aggressive acts such as throwing missiles such as coins at the players on the field or at other supporters with intent to injure them, which was frequently mentioned. However, the number of major incidents at each ground bears some relation to how worried spectators at each ground were.

'It was against Glasgow Rangers. They were throwing bottles and coins and using threatening behaviour. The police were trying to get them off the pitch.'

'It was when they played Chelsea last season. They were spread over the ground. They ran riot, fighting, spitting, swearing. I even was frightened.'

Crushing caused by crowds

Some of the most notorious soccer disasters, such as at Bolton in 1946 and at Ibrox in 1971, have been caused by crowd crushes. While the Bolton disaster was caused partly by the ground being simply too full, the Ibrox tragedy was caused by crowd movement in a limited space. This was one of the most commonly mentioned worries in this category. Although there have been guidelines for some time governing the width of exits and passageways, as discussed in Chapter 4 these guidelines cover only physically dangerous levels, yet even crushing which may not be considered as officially dangerous can be quite frightening.

'At the back of the shelf the gangways became very congested on leaving the match and we felt in sympathy with a sardine.'

A second worry was crowd surges on the terraces. Some people remembered how frightening it was when they were children and could be lifted off the ground by the force of a crowd swaying forward to follow the action on the pitch.

SPECTATORS' VIEWS

Crushing caused by mounted police

Incidents mentioned in this category were of two types. In the first, crowd crushes were caused by mounted police advancing into an enclosed space. As those closest to the horses moved back to get out of the way, those farther back were crowded into limited space, against walls or into small alleyways. Second, as the horses themselves are large animals, some people said they had been frightened or worried by close contact with them.

> 'Celtic v Rangers, [in] a small street leading to the game, a fight started. Police on horseback came. Small children playing in the street could have been hurt.'

It is paradoxical that police action taken to reduce the potential risk from crowd violence should in itself put spectators in what they feel is a dangerous situation. One can imagine that innocent bystanders may be particularly affronted to find themselves crushed because of mounted-police action trying to sort out trouble elsewhere. The dangers associated with policing tactics in an enclosed space are already known. When police used tear gas to dispel rioters in Lima National Stadium, Peru, in 1964, 218 people were killed in the ensuing crush. While a major contributory factor in this disaster was that the stadium doors were locked, the incident still serves as an extreme example of the potential dangers of badly managed crowd control.

Safer parts of the ground

The respondents were asked which parts of their ground were safest. Leaving aside quips such as 'the directors' box' the responses were coded from plans of the stadia as standing at a goal end, standing on the sides, or being seated. The general trend was that the seats were seen as being safest, followed by the sides and then the ends, although there were some interesting differences, such as at Sunderland, where this trend was completely reversed. We will come back later to the question of differences between the seats and the terraces. It would seem though that the seats have a safer image.

Most studies of crowd control at football matches address the issue of seated versus standing accommodation. Seating produces a crowd of uniform, low density and makes observation easier. On the other hand, in less than capacity crowds, troublemakers can be more difficult to reach in seats than they would be on the terraces. We have seen that seats are seen as typically safer than the terraced 'ends'. Is this because of some effect that the provision of seating has on crowd behaviour or because the stands attract a different sort of spectator than the terraces? Some people may be drawn to the stands because they believe them to be safe. Sitting is typically more expensive than standing at matches and we would therefore expect that people of higher socioeconomic status would be likely to sit. This is in fact the case (Fig. 2.9). Those who choose to sit also tend to be older than those who stand. Not surprisingly, they also find the grounds to be more comfortable.

Of more interest are the differences in attitudes between the two groups. Generally, the people who sit are less concerned with their team winning than with watching a good game (Fig. 2.10). They would be more critical of physical violence at a football match (Fig. 2.11) and they would be less likely to think 'taking the mickey' was acceptable (Fig. 2.12). But, although the overall figures are in the direction that supports the hypothesis of a younger, slightly more aggressive, set of people on the terraces, the pattern is far from strong and varies considerably from club to club. One further question illuminates these patterns. We asked whether it would be worth paying a little more for better facilities. The patterns of answers to this will of course be a function of the socioeconomic status of spectators and of how good they think the conditions are already, but beyond the fact that most supporters would like to see better conditions and would be prepared to pay for them, it is clear that those who sit are more likely to want their comforts than those who stand (Fig. 2.13).

What emerges from these comparisons is a picture of older, more staid supporters going to a match to watch a game in comfort as characteristic of those who sit and a tendency in many clubs for those on the terraces to be more youthful and high spirited. There are certainly no surprises here, except that this pattern is not strong and rigidly applicable to all clubs. It also has to be taken against the background of people recognising the terraces as less safe.

What we have here, then, are spectators who think that the conditions at football grounds are quite good but at the same time feel that many improvements could be made, either to the facilities, the fabric of the stadium, or management and players. They also

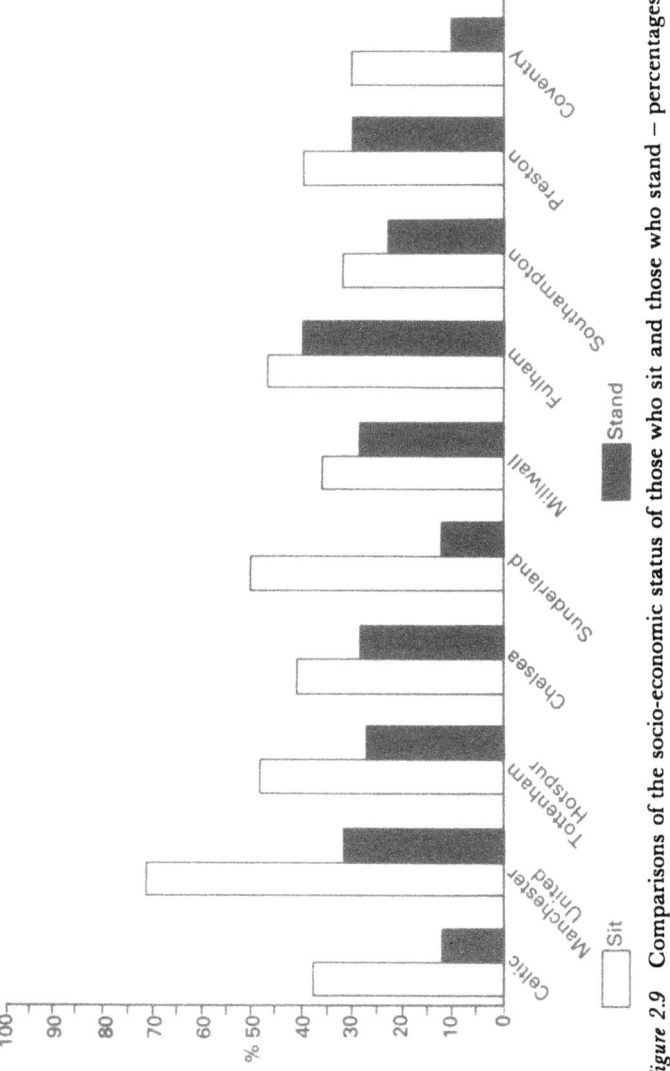

Figure 2.9 Comparisons of the socio-economic status of those who sit and those who stand – percentages of classes A, B, C1.

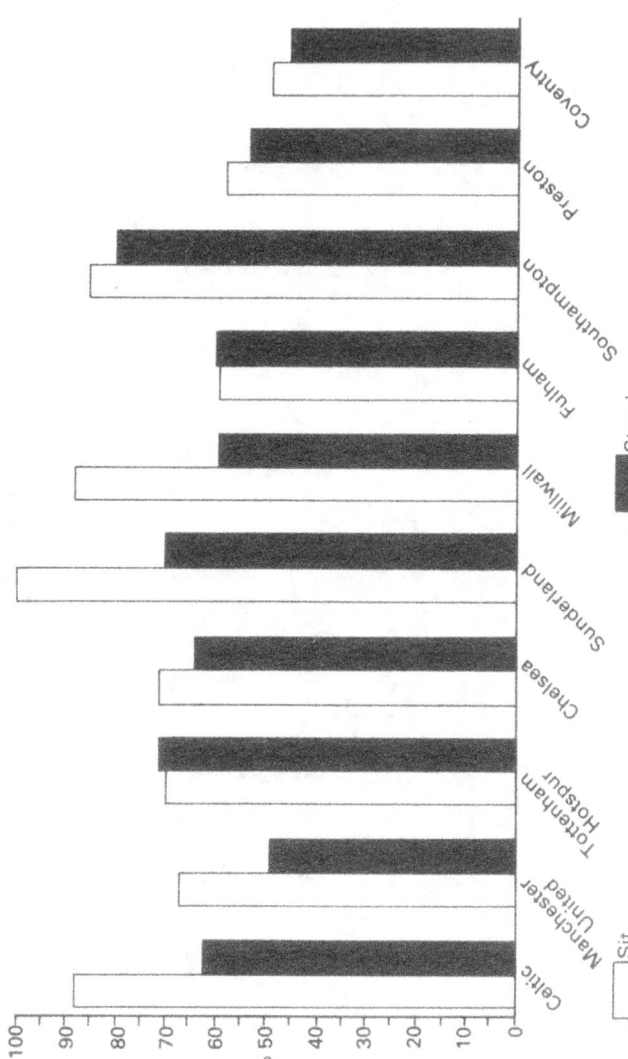

Figure 2.10 Percentages of those who sit and those who stand who agree that an enjoyable game is more important than winning.

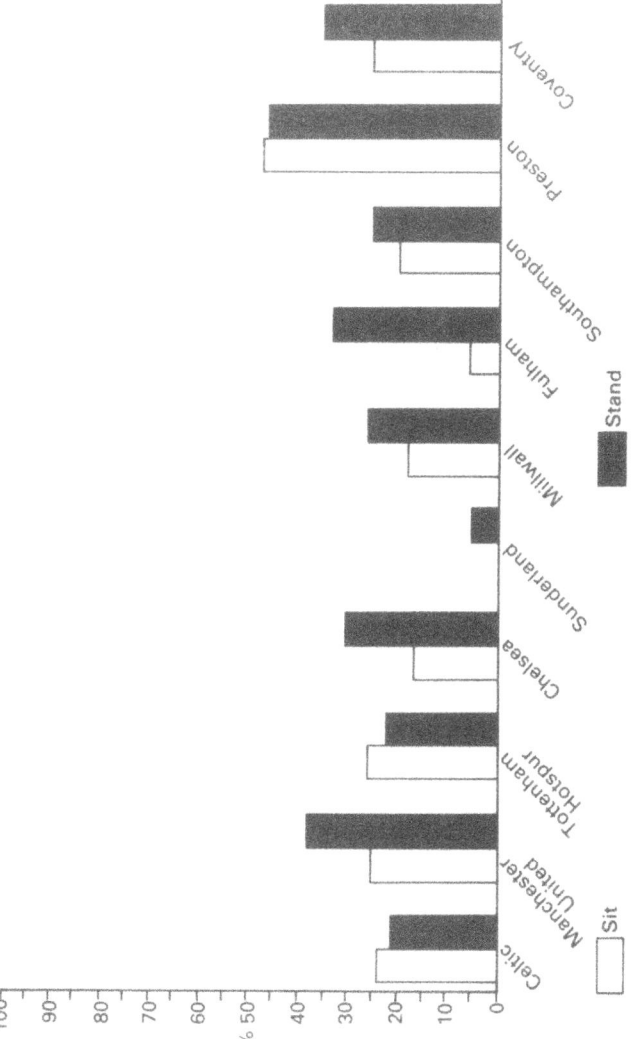

Figure 2.11 Percentages of those who sit and those who stand who agree that "I wouldn't be as critical of physical violence at a football match as I would be in other situations".

Figure 2.12 Percentages of those who sit and those who stand who agree that "It's all right to take the mickey out of other sides' football supporters".

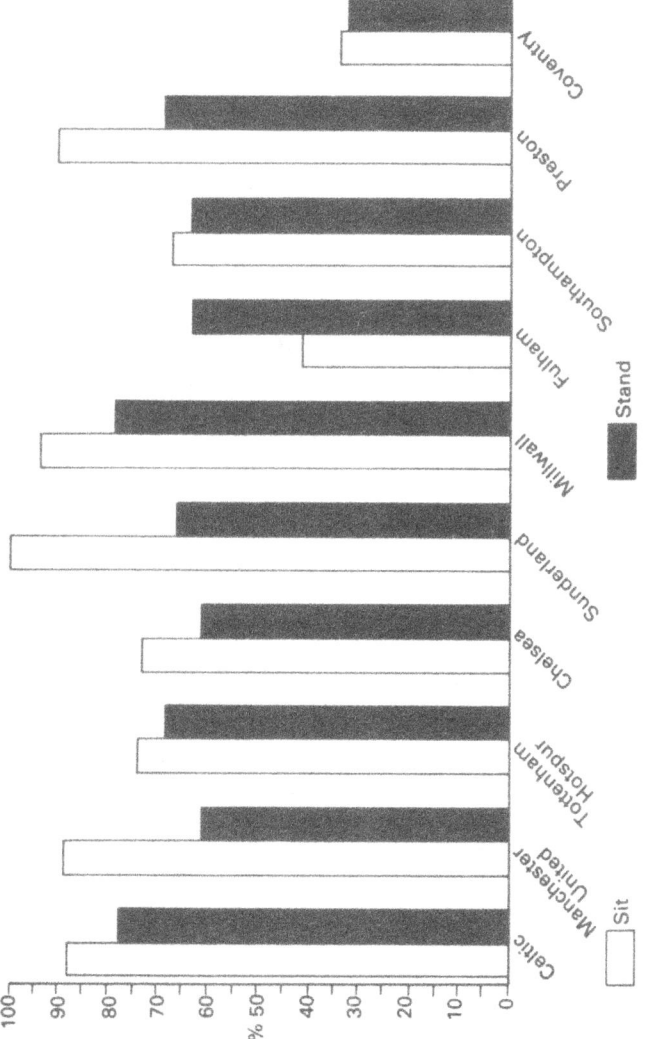

Figure 2.13 Percentages of those who sit and those who stand who would pay more for better facilities.

feel that it would be worth paying at least a little more for these improvements.

We have also highlighted differences in people's attitudes. For example, we have shown that people who prefer seats tend to be older and more interested in comfort and entertainment than those on the terraces. We have suggested that this is related to the general belief that the seats are safe. This belief will encourage those who want to keep away from any possible trouble to congregate together in one area and in turn that area will tend to be quieter because of the type of supporters it attracts, reinforcing the belief that it is safe. Of course, if hooligans moved to the seats en masse then all this might become true of the terraces rather than the seats. Such a move is also a much greater general threat to football. Once even the seats are no longer seen as safe then the whole perception of the grounds goes down a notch. Those affrays in recent years that took place in the seated areas would therefore be expected to be especially threatening to the future of the game.

In the same way that worry about the possibility of trouble may discourage the less committed supporters from going to matches, it is possible that football may be left to those who actively enjoy 'hooliganism' or to those dwindling numbers of supporters who manage to tolerate it because of the strength of their loyalty to the sport. In this situation the level of violence at matches can only increase. Furthermore, any small incident that is given great publicity will be taken by all as evidence for the continuation of the threatening situation they perceive at present.

In conclusion, then, although it is not the whole reason why fewer people attend matches, spectators' concern for their safety at football matches is the most important reason why people stop going to matches. They see crowd violence as the single most significant cause for that concern. In the next chapter we look at what hooliganism actually is, at some of the explanations that have been put forward to account for its existence, and at suggested ways of reducing it.

MEMBERSHIP SCHEMES

Legislation to create membership schemes for football clubs has been introduced since we did our survey. But at that time, as now, it was a highly contentious issue. The proposal was that supporters could register as members of the club they support and be given an identity card as evidence of that membership. If matches were then made ticket-only, or at least restricted to members, the club would have direct control over who can attend their ground. Membership would initially be given to anyone who asks, but anyone who causes trouble could, at the discretion of the management, have their membership withdrawn by repossession or invalidation of their identity card. Thus troublemakers could be excluded at subsequent matches. If all clubs had such programmes then supporters could be admitted to away matches on the basis of membership of their own club. While this would require some co-operation between home and away clubs for each match, the problems should not be insurmountable. More serious difficulties might arise in reliably identifying troublemakers and in making the case for withdrawing a supporter's membership rights. Closed-circuit television would be very useful in these circumstances because, while management could withdraw membership or refuse admission without giving reasons, as is often done in night clubs, concrete evidence that innocent supporters are not being mistakenly barred would be essential for the smooth and peaceful running of such a scheme.

We asked the survey respondents whether they would agree with a membership-card scheme. There was general resistance to the idea, with 62 per cent disagreeing completely. If a membership-card scheme were to be introduced 57 per cent said they would prefer a club system, while 43 per cent would prefer a national system. Some people think that a national scheme is very close to a national identity-card system and they dislike the 'Big Brother' control implied. While it is preferred, a club system may in fact be more difficult to administer, for the simple reason that people follow more than one team. While all clubs had supporters who also watched other clubs play, the percentage of respondents who supported more than one team varied from club to club (Fig. 2.14). This means that some clubs may, possibly, be in favour of club membership schemes where others would only countenance a national membership scheme.

Our results, as submitted to the Popplewell Inquiry, pointed out the great difficulty of ever running a club-based membership scheme across the country. If someone does only watch one club, as is likely to be the case for a Sunderland supporter, then a local club membership may be less irksome. But for someone who watches

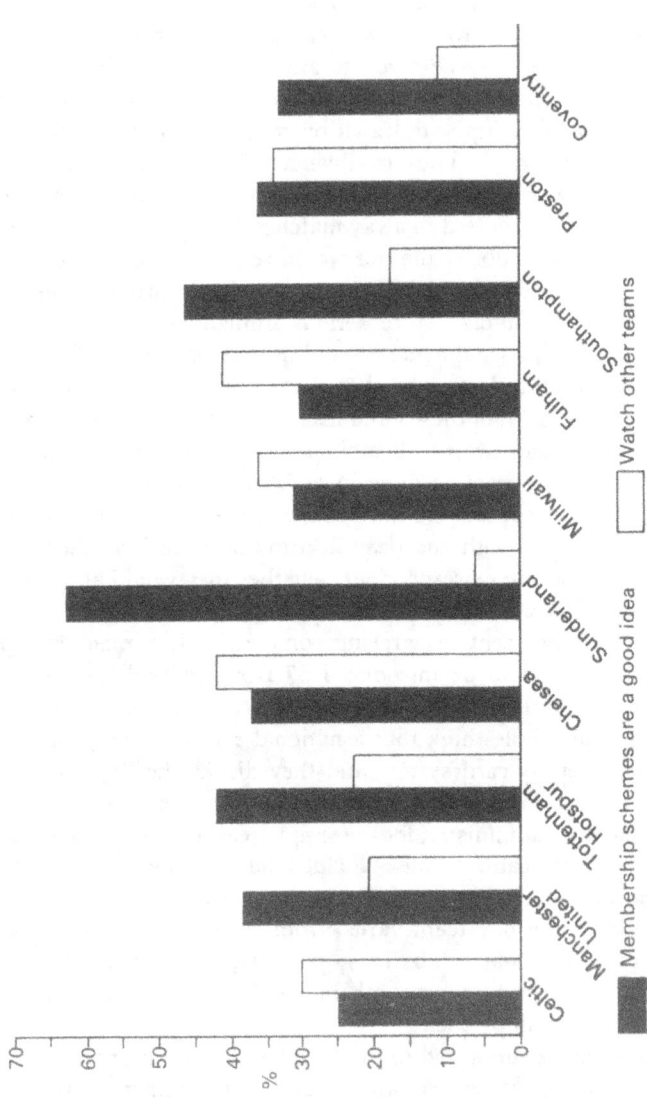

Figure 2.14 Percentages of respondents, at each of ten clubs, who watch other teams and percentages who support membership schemes.

two, three or more clubs such a club-based system gets so complicated and bothersome that many people would almost certainly rather stay at home. Chelsea supporters, for example, named 21 other clubs which they watched. While most interest centred around other London clubs, some supporters watched north of England or Scottish teams (Table 2.1).

The recommendations in the Popplewell report took account of these considerations and the proposal for a national membership scheme was put before parliament. So although the idea of a national scheme appears more feasible than the club schemes that were originally being mooted, the outcry at even that proposal was predictable from our results. Sunderland, after all, was the only club, out of the ten we looked at across the country, where the majority of supporters were in favour of a membership scheme.

Another difficulty with membership schemes is that they discourage casual spectators. If the schemes were strictly enforced, one would no longer be able simply to turn up at a match on the whim of a moment. One would expect, then, that those least in favour of the idea would be the infrequent supporters. In fact, it turns out that the opposite is true. Most opposition came from those fans who go to most games (Fig. 2.15). Those in favour of the schemes are less likely to approve of mickey-taking and more likely to agree to pay more for improved conditions (Figs. 2.16, 2.17). It seems, then, that supporters of membership schemes have a good deal in common with lapsed supporters, in terms of both attitudes and attendance patterns, an observation which does not augur well for the future of the schemes.

Membership schemes have little support and are unlikely to succeed unless provision is made for the numerous football fans who support a number of clubs. At the moment the schemes are not presented as having an immediate benefit to the club member. Unlike most other clubs, members do not get anything extra for joining – the schemes are envisaged purely as exclusion devices. Later on in the book we will argue that football needs a more positive attitude about what belonging to a club means. Perhaps such an attitude would make schemes such as these at least more palatable, if not more easily administered.

FOOTBALL IN ITS PLACE

Table 2:1 Teams watched by more than 3 per cent of each club's supporters

Supporters	Other club watched	%
CHELSEA		
	Tottenham Hotspur	9
	Fulham	9
	Queen's Park Rangers	8
	Manchester United	4
	Wimbledon	4
FULHAM		
	Chelsea	14
	Arsenal	8
	West Ham United	4
	Manchester United	3
	Luton	3
	Queen's Park Rangers	3
	Brentford	3
MILLWALL		
	Arsenal	9
	Tottenham Hotspur	9
	Charlton	7
	Chelsea	5
	West Ham United	4
	Crystal Palace	4
PRESTON		
	Liverpool	10
	Manchester United	5
	Tranmere Rovers	4
CELTIC		
	Rangers	16
	Clyde	5
	Partick Thistle	4
TOTTENHAM HOTSPUR		
	Chelsea	4
	West Ham United	3
	Arsenal	3
MANCHESTER UNITED		
	Manchester City	7
	Stockport County	3
	Oldham Athletic	3
SOUTHAMPTON		
	Manchester United	4
	Liverpool	4
	Portsmouth	3
	Everton	3
	Tottenham Hotspur	3
COVENTRY		
	Birmingham City	3
	Leicester City	2

No more than 2 per cent of Sunderland supporters watched another team. Those teams were Manchester United, Newcastle United and Liverpool.

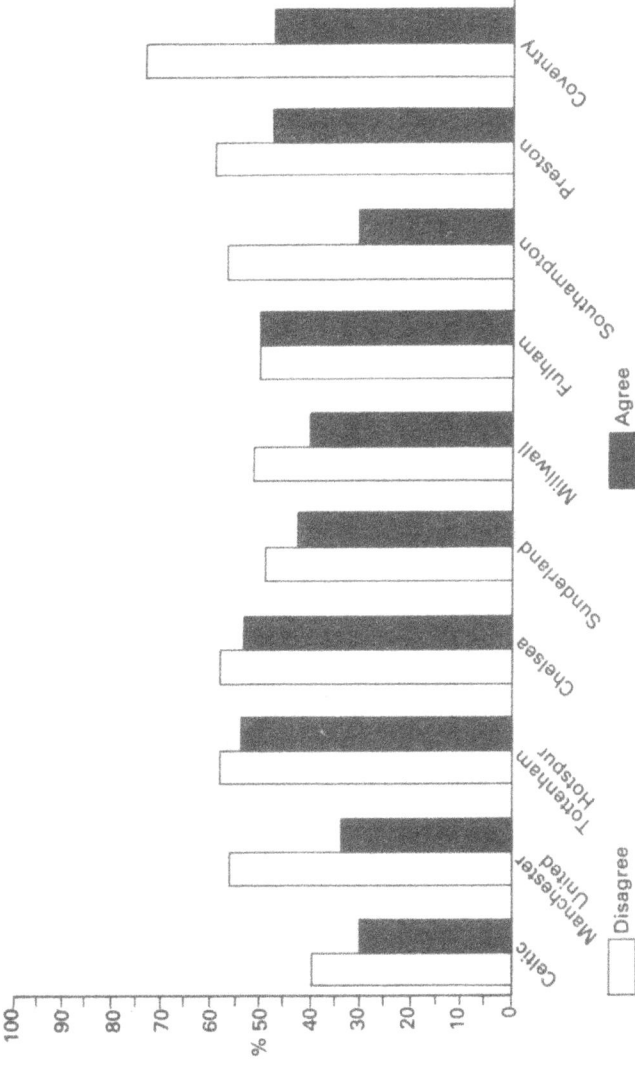

Figure 2.15 Percentages of respondents, at each of ten clubs, who go/went to most matches who agree/disagree with membership card schemes.

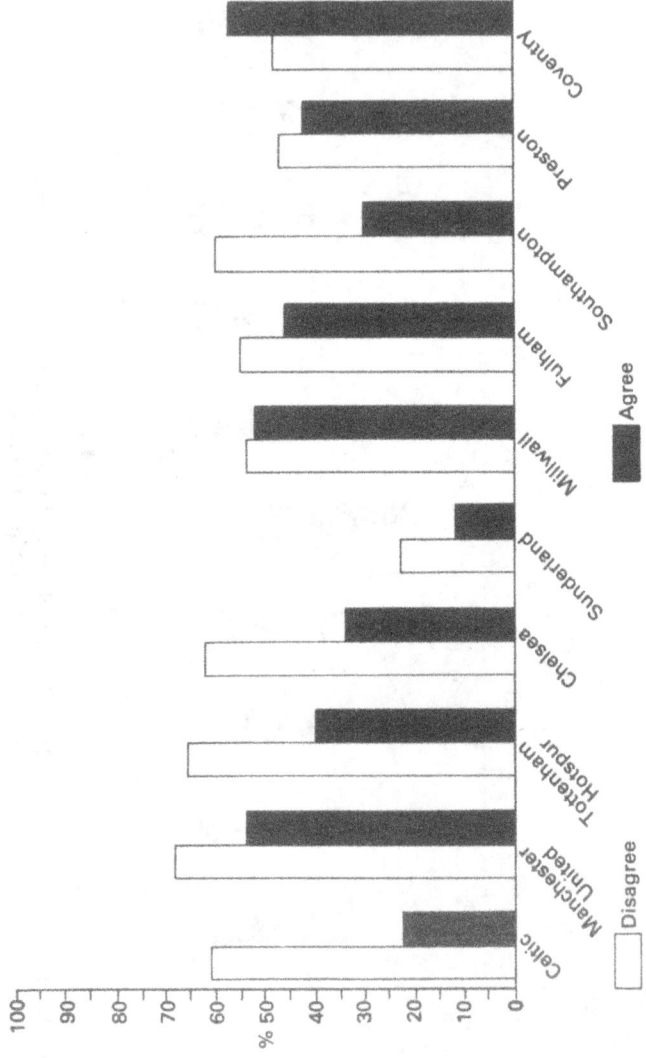

Figure 2.16 Percentages of respondents, at each of ten clubs, who agree with the statement: "It's all right to take the mickey out of other sides' football supporters", who agree/disagree with membership card schemes.

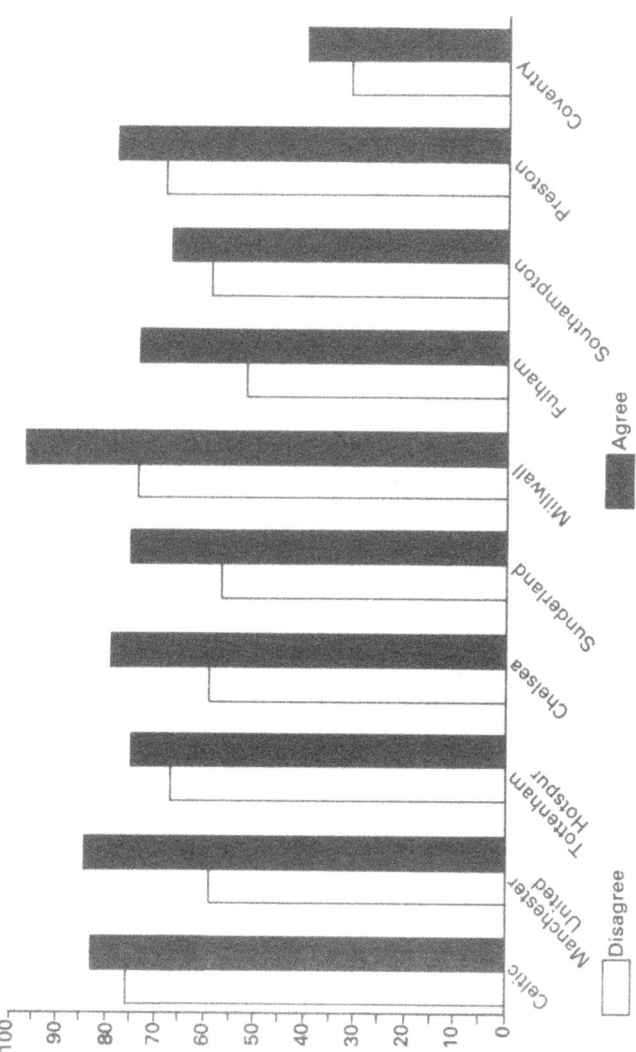

Figure 2.17 Percentages of respondents, at each of ten clubs, who think it would be worth paying a little more if facilities at the ground were better, who agree/disagree with membership card schemes.

FOOTBALL IN ITS PLACE

SUMMARY

This chapter has been concerned with turning the spotlight on football's 'man in the street', the spectator. We want to show that the opinions of the supporter have as much worth as those of the experts who are often called on to contribute to debates on the present state and possible future of football. We have also pointed out, however, that the views of spectators must be tapped in a systematic way, both to avoid bias and to ensure that the summary we present does justice to the varieties of opinion which exist within so large a group.

Of the areas touched on by our survey, three have been highlighted in this chapter: the physical conditions encountered at grounds, the differences which emerge between clubs, and the recurring emphasis on hooliganism.

It appears that some degree of comfort and reasonable facilities are important to spectators. In particular, although many supporters felt that their home ground compared favourably to others, two-thirds of supporters would like at least some improvement and about the same proportion felt that these improvements would encourage more people to go to matches.

We have found that the climate of opinion varies from club to club. For example, when we looked at attitudes toward seating, Coventry supporters usually disagreed with supporters from other clubs. As Coventry was the only club to have had an 'all-seater' experiment, this difference of opinion has obvious roots. Variations in attitude from one club to another caution us against treating football supporters, or football clubs, as one homogeneous group. We will look more closely at the variation between clubs in the next chapter where we suggest that these differences add up to a unique culture at each club.

Spectators seem to be worried about their safety from violence at matches, to a disturbing degree. Hooliganism is also cited as a reason why people give up going to football matches. We therefore turn, in Chapter 5, to an examination of hooliganism. We will look at how social scientists, among others, have tried to explain the phenomenon and at the implications these explanations have for a long-term solution to the problem.

Chapter Three

CLUB CULTURES

Ask any fan about the differences between his club and others and he can tell you. It seems obvious to supporters that clubs vary widely, that each has its own 'personality'. Ask most outsiders and, while they can see that clubs come in various sizes and have varying success, they would be at a loss to see any uniqueness. After all, players and managers move from one club to another and back again. One club's new star player may have been doing his best to score against them last season. When people talk about football's falling gates, a lone cry of 'our attendance went up' can be easily hidden amidst the general shouts of soccer is becoming less popular, getting more dangerous, and so on. Most of the discussion about soccer takes it to be a single monolithic entity.

Of course, clubs do have a lot in common with each other. But the view of their homogeneity also seems to feed a desire for neatness. If football is homogeneous then all clubs will have similar problems, and solutions to those problems should be applicable with equal success to all clubs. Any attempts to find a standard panacea is likely to be met with the comment, 'Nice idea but it won't work here', because simple solutions ignore the individuality of the clubs.

The differences we are talking about here are more than just differences in size, wealth or geographical position, although of course these come into it. More interesting and at the heart of soccer's problems are differences in what might be called the 'ethos' of clubs. Some clubs are perceived as friendly, some as impressive, some as apathetic and some as hostile. These are the types of characteristic which can easily be described anecdotally but which are notoriously difficult to pin down. In this chapter we attempt to do just that, by looking at the patterns of attendance, commitment and attitudes to football across the ten clubs in our sample.

DIFFERENCES IN ATTENDANCE PATTERN AND COMMITMENT

There are a number of clubs, not always First Division sides but often wealthy and prestigious, which regularly attract gates of 30,000 or more. It does not necessarily follow that they have the most committed supporters. A crowd of 30,000 can be produced by 90,000 supporters who come to 1 game in 3 or by 30,000 supporters who never miss. Looking at sheer numbers gives a poorer measure of commitment than looking at the percentage of supporters who turn up regularly to cheer from the terraces. In our survey we were able to look at which clubs have relatively high proportions of committed supporters and at whether there are different types of commitment to be found in each club.

About half of the 965 supporters interviewed said they went to most games. This proportion varied somewhat but not greatly across clubs. The club that had the most committed supporters in our sample was Coventry, where 66 per cent of respondents said they went to most games. The least committed was Celtic with 40 per cent (Fig. 3.1). Yet this is not the whole story, for by contrast 69 per cent of Celtic supporters travel to away matches but only 37 per cent of Coventry supporters do (Fig. 3.2). Just over a quarter of the Coventry supporters had season tickets whereas only 4 per cent of Celtic supporters did (Fig. 3.3). Twenty three per cent of Celtic supporters had been to see their team play abroad, in contrast to only 4 per cent of Coventry supporters (Fig. 3.4). The two clubs seem to offer good examples of different types of support. In Coventry's case there is a high level of local commitment, of supporting the team at home, shown by regular attendance and the longer-term commitment of buying a season ticket. In contrast, Celtic supporters are travellers, they are the fans most likely to watch their club play away, more so than supporters of other clubs who have more than one team in their city. Given more opportunities for foreign travel than Coventry, Celtic fans are also most likely to watch their team play abroad. They are, however, not such reliable fans at home.

Spurs supporters come somewhere between these two, showing

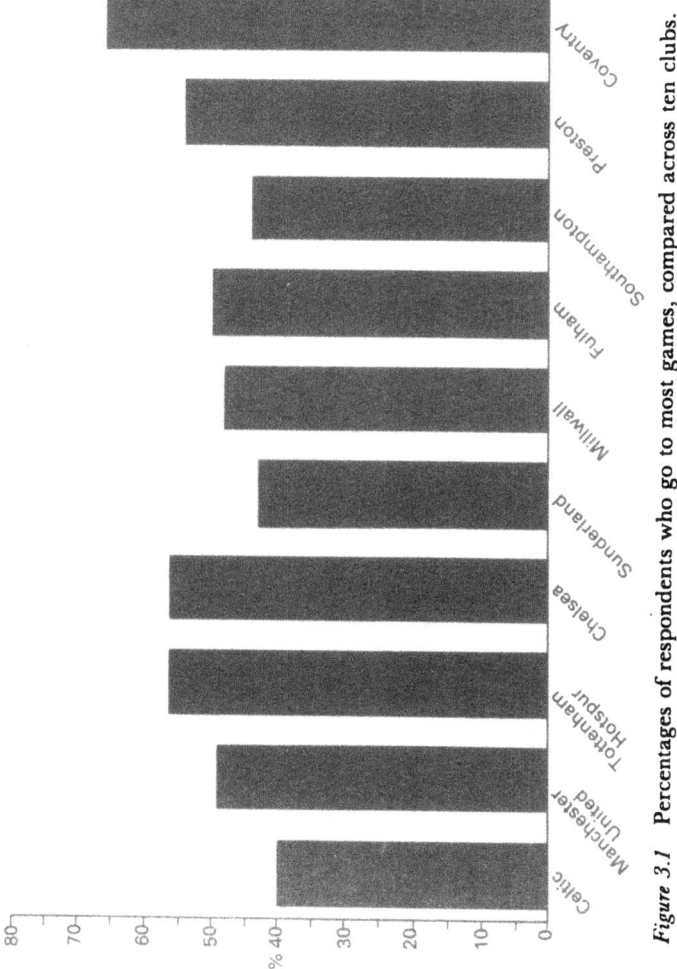

Figure 3.1 Percentages of respondents who go to most games, compared across ten clubs.

Figure 3.2 Percentages of respondents who go to away games, at each of ten clubs.

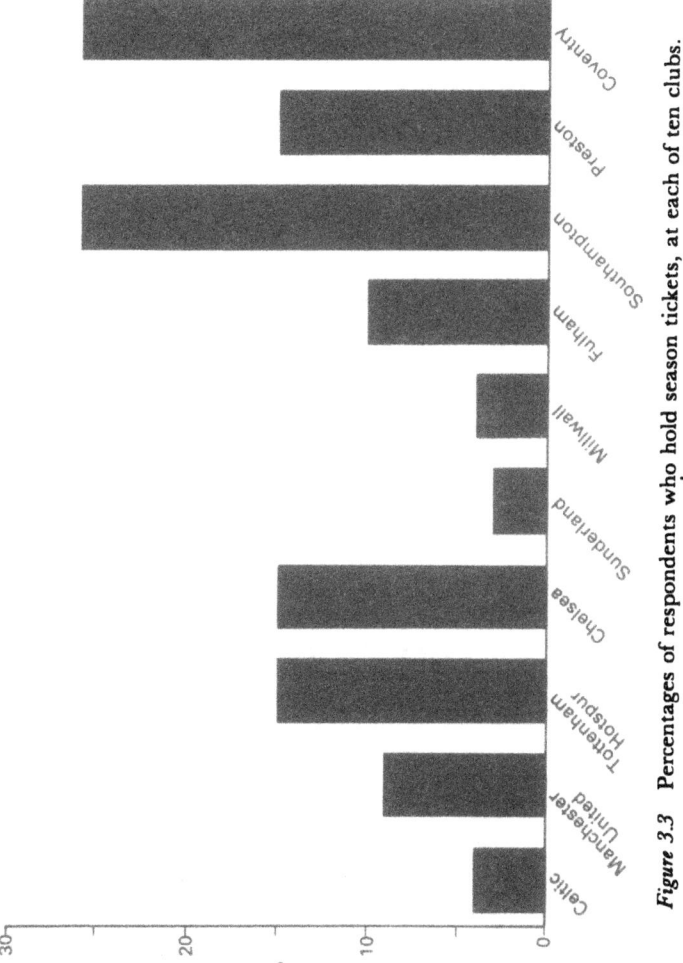

Figure 3.3 Percentages of respondents who hold season tickets, at each of ten clubs.

Figure 3.4 Percentages of respondents who have seen their team play abroad, at each of ten clubs.

moderate levels of attendance at both home and away matches, travelling abroad and buying season tickets. Spurs fans have the advantage of following a successful London team that has many local First Division rivals, so that many of the team's away matches are relatively easily accessible. Compared with the other London clubs in our sample, Spurs supporters watch other teams least. Chelsea and Fulham supporters watched other teams most often. Distance is obviously critical as it was most often the neighbouring team that was watched, with Chelsea fans watching Fulham and Fulham fans Chelsea.

There would seem, therefore, to be at least two types of supporters, locals and travellers. While all clubs will have some of each, some clubs, because of tradition, geographical position or success rate, may have a preponderance of one or the other.

DIFFERENCES IN ATTITUDES

As well as asking supporters what they did (how often they went to matches or how many other teams they watched) we also asked them what they thought. We have already considered supporters' views on the physical conditions at grounds in Chapter 2. We can now look at the differences between clubs. Since grounds differ in size, age, capacity and state of repair, we would expect people's opinions of them to vary from ground to ground as well. The importance of these opinions is that a football stadium is not just an open-air building but probably the most enduring symbol of the home team.

We also examined from two angles supporters' attitudes towards the event of watching football. First, we asked about events at their home ground; the use of obscene language and racist chants; the involvement of political groups and whether they had been worried for their personal safety. The issue of safety had been discussed in Chapter 2, where we pointed out that there were noticeable differences across clubs in how worried their supporters were. Second, we asked respondents to agree or disagree with a number of statements which represented possible views about going to football, about which aspects of watching a match are most important and about the acceptability of verbal and physical aggression between rival fans. All three of these aspects of attitudes, ratings of the home ground, views on the events which take place at the ground, and opinions about going to football, combine to produce an idea of what it is like to be a home supporter at a certain ground.

It might be said that people go to football matches to watch football and that what really matters is the standard of play on the pitch, the team and how it is managed. Therefore, how people feel about their club will be influenced first and foremost by these things. While this may be so, these are not the only aspects to play a role in defining the identity of the club. It is also true to say that both the intangibles, such as club history and traditions and the 'feel' of a club and the physical reality of the ground, will change probably less often than the manager and certainly more slowly than the composition of the team. They therefore make a major contribution to the enduring qualities of the club. So when people start to support, say, Tottenham Hotspur, their experience of 'what it is to be a Spurs supporter' and of actually being at White Hart Lane are just as important as their perceptions of events on the pitch. Unfortunately, these are also the aspects which are least often discussed or studied. We will highlight some of these differences between clubs.

The ground

We have already touched on supporters' perceptions of the grounds in Chapter 2. We can now look in more detail at the differences between clubs. The atmosphere at football grounds varies considerably and is often described in glowing terms. Brian Inglis, in his book *Football Grounds of England and Wales*, calls Old Trafford 'a cave of red and white aggression'.[1] Grounds may be impressive, cosy, tatty or depressing. These overall images of stadia are made up of numerous facets and can be difficult to measure without an in-depth study of people's reactions and perceptions. We didn't have the option of allowing our respondents a completely free rein and so looked at essential points: Was the ground comfortable? How did it compare to other grounds? Did it need improvement?

Most of our respondents watched the game standing on the terraces (Fig. 3.5). The exception was Coventry, where the proportion of the ground given over to seats is high, and only 30 per cent stood. Generally speaking, however, over three-quarters of the respondents stood and so the following comments should be seen in that light.

For people who do not follow football the idea that cold, wet,

Figure 3.5 Percentages of respondents who normally stand, at each of ten clubs.

windblown and litter-strewn terraces are comfortable may come as something of a shock. But those who frequent them say that they are moderately comfortable (19 per cent), quite comfortable (48 per cent) or even comfortable (21 per cent) (Fig. 3.6). If respondents at all clubs rated their grounds as equally comfortable one might suspect that this was a defensive reaction, protesting too much, as it were. Instead, there is variation. Coventry and Fulham are rated as very comfortable and Preston and Celtic less so. Apparently comfort is a relative concept. This question was approached within the framework of what one can reasonably expect of an outdoor sport. If one wants to stand outside for two hours in mid-winter, then the overall level of comfort one expects is less than would be expected in a cinema. Therefore, to say that a football terrace is very comfortable is judging it in context.

The question which seemed to bear a better relation to the level of maintenance and the state of the fabric of the ground was whether respondents thought that physical conditions, rather than comfort, were above or below average (Fig. 3.7). Overall more respondents thought that their ground was above average than below. The top three rated clubs were Manchester United, Coventry City and Tottenham Hotspur and the bottom three were Sunderland, Millwall and Southampton. In other words ratings seem to depend on the size and condition of the ground.

The picture of general complacency suggested by the comfort ratings changes when we consider improvements to the ground (Fig. 3.8). Eighty-three per cent of Celtic supporters and 81 per cent of Millwall supporters thought their ground needed improvement. In fact, the lowest percentage was 40 per cent at Manchester United.

These three questions address three different aspects of supporters' satisfaction with their local stadium. We can now look at how the clubs are rated on all three in conjunction (Table 3.1).

Table 3.1 Ratings given to the physical conditions at each ground

	Man	Cov	Spu	Ful	Chel	Sund	Mill	Pres	Cel	Sou
Comfort	***	***	**	***	**	**	***	*	*	*
Conditions	***	***	***	**	***	*	*	**	**	*
Improvements	***	***	**	**	*	***	*	**	*	**

*** Very good
** Medium
* Poor

Figure 3.6 Percentages of respondents who think the ground is comfortable, at each of ten clubs.

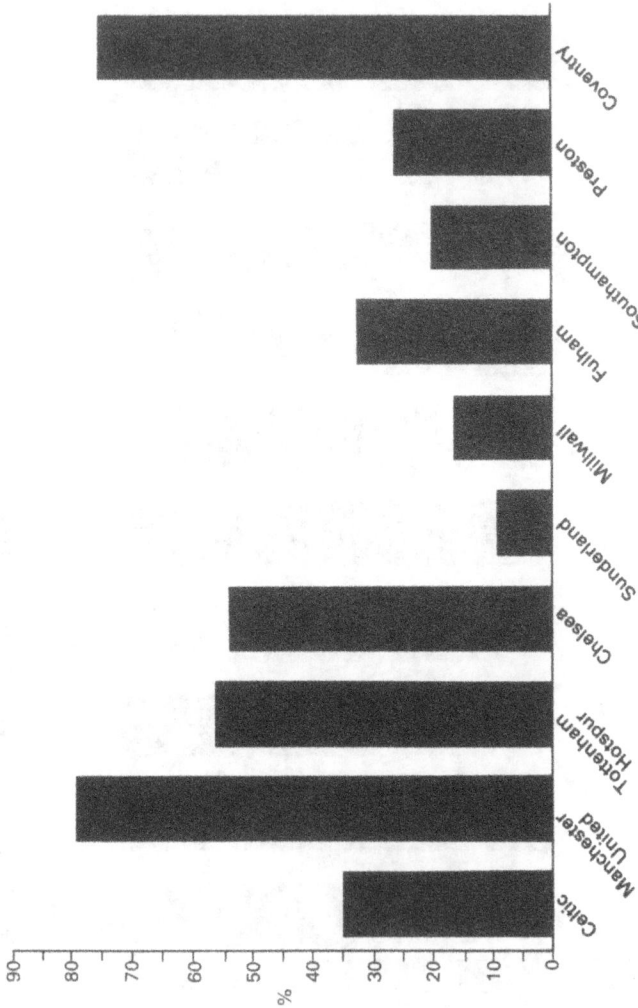

Figure 3.7 Percentages of respondents who think conditions are above average, at each of ten clubs.

Figure 3.8 Percentages of respondents who think that improvements are needed, at each of ten clubs.

Manchester United and Coventry come top of the list with high ratings all round. Other clubs, such as Millwall, have more mixed ratings suggesting in this case that the respondents can see that the conditions are not ideal but do not let this affect their overall assessment of the ground.

STYLE OF SUPPORT

A second aspect which contributes to the feel of a particular club is the style of support it attracts. This can be expressed in many different ways but one of the most noticeable is the views that supporters have on what is appropriate by way of chants and shouts. From outside the crowd the most noticeable feature is the sheer noise. From inside the words become clearer and more salient. When these chants and shouts are obscene, vulgar or insulting, does it matter? Or do outsiders interpret these chants wrongly by taking them out of context?

Bawling, shouting, cursing, swearing

Although Liverpool is supposedly the home of most chants, the repertoire from which chants and songs are taken seems to be common to all clubs. Many of these chants use obscene language and some are openly racist. For many people 'rich' language is part and parcel of what goes on at soccer matches. This is, after all, still predominantly a male pursuit and 'minding your language' is traditionally associated with mixed-sex gatherings. On the other hand some people may find this language extremely offensive. It seemed that people's attitudes towards the use of obscene language might be one indication of how 'rough' a club was.

Figure 3.9 shows, first, the percentage of people who thought that there was a lot of obscene language at their local ground and, second, the percentage who were worried by this. The percentage who reported a lot of swearing varies considerably, from 68 per cent at Celtic to 18 per cent at Fulham. While the percentage who expressed their dislike of the amount of swearing also varies, it is immediately apparent that this number is relatively small. It does seem, then, that 'bad language' is accepted as part of the football event – it is part of what goes on at a match and not really something to worry about. The strength, or weakness, of disapproval varies

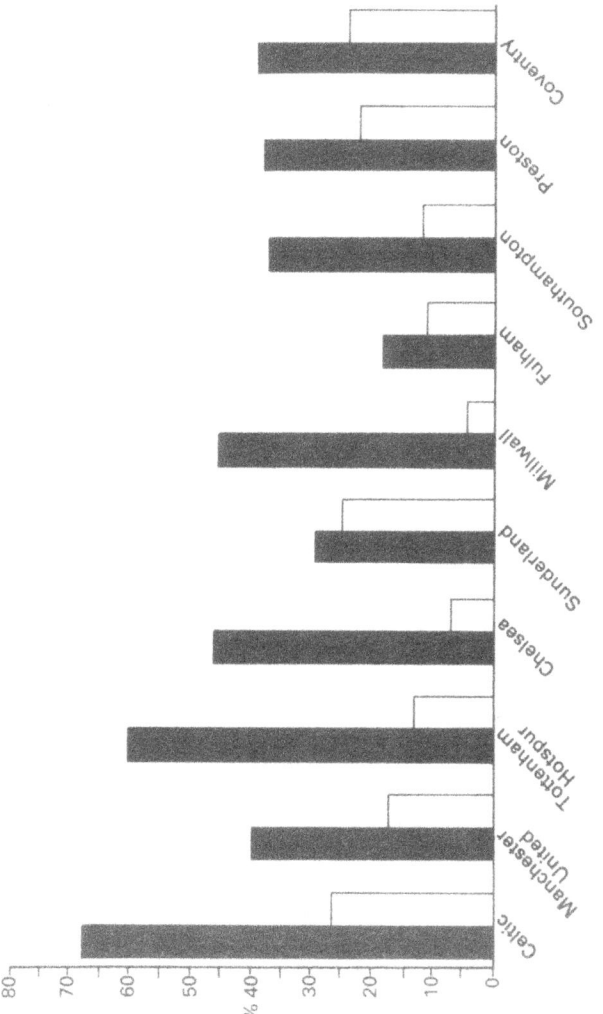

Figure 3.9 Percentages of respondents who agreed that they heard a lot of obscene language, and percentages who were worried by any bad language, at each of ten clubs.

from club to club, i.e. the gap between the two figures differs. For example, 39 per cent report a lot of bad language at Coventry and over half that number (24 per cent) dislike it. At Millwall, however, 45 per cent say that there is a lot of swearing but only 4 per cent, less than one-tenth, disapprove. So, while swearing is accepted overall, feelings about it depend to some extent on the club.

Racism and fascism

Figure 3.10 compares the percentage who say there are a lot of racist chants at their ground with the percentage who are worried by them. Also included is the percentage of supporters who said that political groups are involved at their ground. Here, the picture is totally different from that for 'bad language'. With the exception of Celtic, more people are worried by racist chants than think they hear a lot of them; people are even worried by what they themselves think is a low incidence of racially prejudiced chants. Football supporters are seemingly less tolerant of open racism than of swearing. Most chants are heard at Celtic (66 per cent) and fewest at Fulham (15 per cent). Fulham are also most worried about the chants (64 per cent) and Celtic the least (25 per cent).

If we go on to look at political involvement we find that Celtic comes in the bottom three at 39 per cent and, further, that the group involved is not the National Front or the British Movement but the IRA. Here we come across one major cross-club difference based on the local and regional history of a club. In Glasgow the great rivalry between Celtic and Rangers is based on the religious and ethnic origins of the two clubs, with Celtic being Irish Catholic down to its team colours and Rangers Scottish Protestant. We must suppose that this gives rise not only to racism at Celtic Park but also to its acceptance as part of the traditional rivalries of their football scene.

On the other hand, racism in England tends to be focused on blacks, Asians and Jews. The English club where most racist chanting was reported was Chelsea. Many respondents also thought that political groups, for example the National Front, were active at Chelsea. However, Chelsea supporters are not complacent about this position. Just over half the supporters interviewed were worried by racist chanting.

Worry about openly expressed racism is not necessarily related

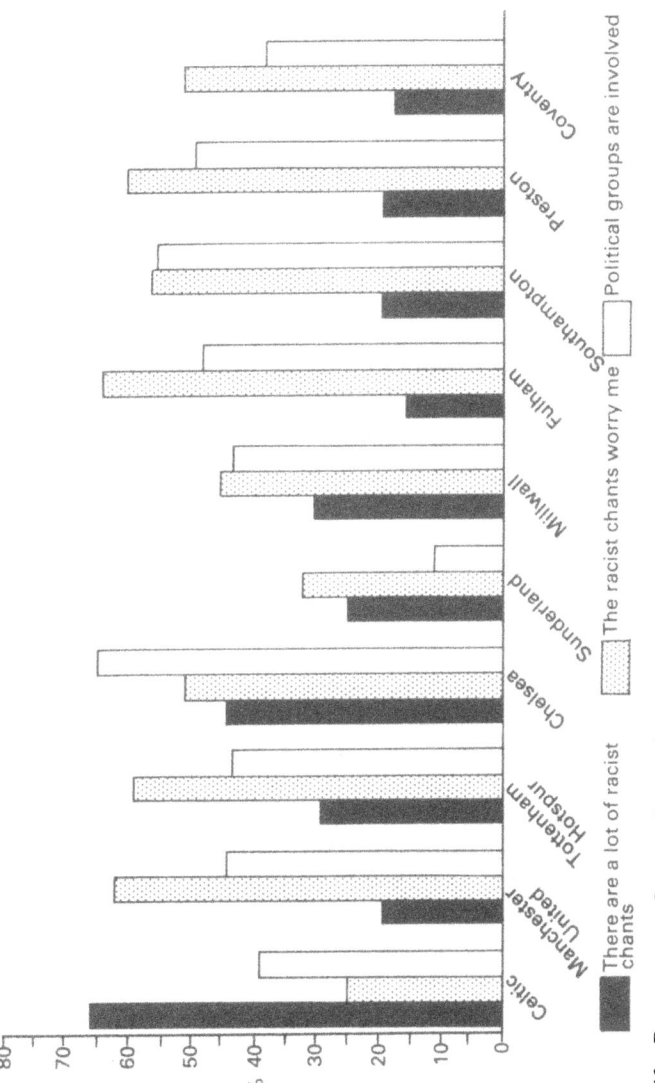

Figure 3.10 Percentages of respondents who agree "there are a lot of racist shouts or chants", and who agree "the racist shouts or chants do worry me", at each of ten clubs.

to the amount reported. Some of the clubs where fewest said there were racist chants were most worried by the level they did report. Here the results can be seen to fit also into the overall pattern of variations across clubs, but more detailed examination would be necessary to establish how representative our sample of supporters were for each individual club.

ATTITUDES

Our earlier discussion of the opinions and commitment of supporters gives an account of some aspects of their attitudes. But this account is somewhat oblique. It is quite feasible to ask people directly about their views on various matters and so reveal their attitudes from their own comments. Asking such questions is a fine art, in order to avoid bias and avoid people simply giving what they think will be an acceptable answer.

For our survey of football supporters we did find a number of questions that were subtle enough to reveal differences between clubs. To generate these questions we used the time-honoured procedure of listing statements that are typical of those used by our respondents and then asking them if they agreed or disagreed with those statements. The percentage of supporters who express agreement is then a useful indication of the attitudes of that group of supporters.

In all we had thirteen statements that were presented to all respondents. Their answers do reveal a number of interesting differences between groups of supporters. They go a lot further to support our general point that there are indeed large variations between clubs in the attitudinal culture that is created by their supporters.

In Chapter 2 some of the responses to the attitudinal statements were presented in order to help our understanding of the differences between lapsed and regular supporters and between supporters who choose to sit and those who choose to stand. In order to look a little more closely at the attitudinal differences we will turn to the regular supporters for each of the ten clubs.

In looking at the attitudinal differences it is important to be aware of the relationships between different attitudes. Until now we have discussed supporters' attitudes to the club as if each were entirely independent. In fact, opinions about a particular issue are more usually part of a constellation of attitudes. This is accepted in everyday life, where we expect people to show some consistency across a number of issues. Thus, if someone is an anti-bloodsport hunt saboteur, then we will expect that they will not wear fox-fur coats and perhaps that they will advocate 'health' foods. If someone votes Conservative we expect them to support private enterprise and public schools. We are sometimes wrong in our assumptions about these consistencies. We may make inferences about people's likely attitude or behaviour in any situation from what we know of them already and find that their actual behaviour comes as a surprise. The reason for this discrepancy can be that we have grouped together attitudes which are not, in fact, closely related to each other at all. A person may have sympathy with wild foxes only and class fur from farmed foxes along with sheepskins and leather shoes as acceptable products. The interest lies in finding which attitudes belong in which constellations, which go together in meaningful groups and which groups allow us to distinguish between different types of people. If our Conservative voter chooses to send his child to a comprehensive school we may question whether we should have included school preference in this particular group of attitudes.

In our case we are looking at differences not between people but between football clubs. There were differences between the clubs on the answers their supporters gave to each of thirteen questions. Now we want to see whether there was any pattern in these differences that would make them easier to conceptualise in a more global way. In other words, can we group these questions together so that we can say, for example, these questions are all about comfort, these are about winning, and these about facilities? Of course, we could do this by discussing the questions amongst ourselves and deciding which groupings seemed appropriate. It is more fruitful, however, to use the respondents' views. If we find that people who think seating is important also want weather-proofing and some even want footrests, then we can argue that these three hypothetical items belong together in a group labelled 'the importance of comfort'. If we also find that those who think that winning is important also think that all the club's money should go to buy good players and, further, that they do not care whether the stands fall down as a result, we can put items addressing these issues in the 'importance of winning' category. Now, instead of looking for differences between clubs on one item at a time we can look for differences in the importance accorded to comfort or to winning.

FOOTBALL IN ITS PLACE

In the present case the different aspects of the constellation of attitudes are quite well reflected in just three representative statements. In other words the differences between the clubs are most clearly shown by concentrating on three of the thirteen attitudinal statements. These statements were chosen because they represent key constituents of the variety of attitudes explored. To reiterate, what we mean by 'key constituents' here, put simply, is that all the attitudes were found to relate to each other. So, a few carefully selected statements can be taken as representative of the whole 'system' of attitudes.

The connections between the attitudes were established by the use of advanced statistical procedures[2] that it would be beyond the scope of this book to elaborate. None the less, consideration of the three statements that we will focus on will help to make clear the range of attitudes explored.

Consider, for example, the statement, 'It's alright to take the mickey out of the other side's football supporters.' People who agree with this statement also tend to agree with the statement, 'You expect to see a bit of trouble as part of going to a football match.' Clearly both these statements reflect attitudes about the rumbustious, lively give-and-take at a football match. They were carefully phrased to avoid any indication of a pejorative view and so encourage people to admit to aspects of the slightly aggressive nature of crowds at football matches that they might otherwise have denied.

The statement on 'mickey-taking' deals with a very different attitude from the statement, 'Sitting in reasonable comfort and watching a good game is as important as my team winning.' This deals with the enjoyment of the game rather than with aspects of the crowd. Its significance can be further seen from the fact that agreements with this statement are highly correlated to agreements with the statement, 'Football is more about entertainment than about winning.'

A third statement adds another aspect. This is the statement, 'It's alright for teams to share the same home ground.' This statement relates closely to the statement, 'Clubs could do more to encourage families to go to matches.' It really picks up attitudes towards the social aspects and community connections of a club, rather than emphasising its relationship with a particular team.

These three statements, then, can be taken to illustrate three components of the overall set of attitudes. For simplicity we can refer to these as:

(a) acceptance of mickey-taking
(b) importance of comfort
(c) endorsement of sharing of grounds

Now, in looking at the reactions of different clubs across these three components it is necessary to bear in mind what they already have. Clearly a club that is already sharing its ground with another, or one that has a sumptuously comfortable ground, would have supporters whose attitudes reflected these circumstances. For example, those who had comfort may not regard it as very important any more. It could be that clubs that shared their grounds did so because their supporters were happy with this, or the reverse could be true. Supporters could have accepted a decision that they originally did not agree with. The point is that the causes and consequences of these attitudes cannot be derived in any simple fashion from knowing what the attitudes are.

In order to discover the causes or consequences of the attitudes held by club supporters a more detailed study would be necessary than the one we have been able to carry out. None the less, we can establish the nature of the differences that exist at present. These differences do provide a useful insight into club differences and emphasise the value of future study of these matters.

Table 3.2 Percentage of regular supporters from the ten clubs agreeing with each of three statements

	(a) Acceptance of mickey-taking	(b) Importance of comfort	(c) Endorsement of sharing of grounds
Sunderland	14	71	100
Southampton	43	79	55
Preston	50	47	58
Coventry	50	51	25
Fulham	56	61	41
Chelsea	56	61	39
Millwall	63	67	40
Spurs	64	65	33
Celtic	64	57	28
Manchester United	65	40	23

In Table 3.2 the percentage of regular supporters who agreed with each of the three statements has been listed for all ten clubs. At the top of the table it is very clear that Sunderland hold mickey-taking in low regard and that this is balanced by an emphasis on comfort and the fact that 100 per cent of those interviewed were happy to share a ground. The attitudinal culture of this club and the way its supporters see it as a part of their community entertainment is very clear.

The contrast with Manchester United is graphic. Compared with the 14 per cent of Sunderland supporters who agreed with mickey-taking there are 65 per cent of Manchester United supporters. Compared with the 71 per cent who emphasised comfort there are 40 per cent at Manchester United. Compared with the 100 per cent of Sunderland supporters willing to share a ground there are only 23 per cent at Manchester United. Clearly this is a club in which the culture is linked to a robust support of the club team and its focus on winning.

Between these two extremes the clubs have been ordered in terms of their gradations from the community orientation of Sunderland through to the team orientation of Manchester United. Near to Sunderland but not very close are Southampton and Preston. They are not very keen on sharing the ground but have moderately high percentages agreeing with the statement on mickey-taking. The subtleties of these attitudes can be gauged, however, from the fact that Southampton has the highest proportion of people who believe that sitting in reasonable comfort is as important as the team winning. Their 79 per cent agreement compares with 71 per cent for Sunderland.

At the bottom of the table Spurs and Celtic have patterns that are very similar to Manchester United. Their main difference lies in a rather higher agreement with the need for comfort. This could reflect the overall feeling at Manchester United that their ground is a very comfortable one. However, despite the variations within the groups the distinctions between Sunderland, Southampton and Preston on the one hand and between Spurs, Celtic and Manchester United on the other are very striking. One could well imagine that their supporters go to football matches for very different reasons and would probably not agree with each other on the main criteria to be considered when evaluating an effective football club or acceptable football grounds.

Fulham, Chelsea and Millwall, interestingly three of our London clubs, sit together in our table and are quite close to our fourth London club, Spurs. This is because they all have a similar pattern in terms of moderately high agreement with the acceptability of mickey-taking and moderately low preparedness to share the ground, yet the significance of comfort is higher for them than for Celtic or Manchester United but lower than for Sunderland or Southampton. This is a different sort of, hybrid, culture. A desire for robust comfort may be an appropriate way of describing this group. One could see them shouting abuse at their opponents from the comfort of their padded seats.

Coventry has a curiously distinct profile. Most of the clubs that are low on mickey-taking are higher on sharing and vice versa. Yet Coventry supporters' endorsement of mickey-taking is in the middle at 50 per cent but their desire to share is one of the lowest at 25 per cent. There may well be local circumstances that would explain this difference, or as in all these data this may be one of the artefacts of our relatively small samples.

The attitudinal material, then, is very intriguing. It does show that we can identify reasonably subtle differences in some of the attitudes that are at the heart of going to football matches. The initial inquiry was not really set up to explore these attitudinal differences so we were only able to make a first stab at examining these matters. However, the fact that such differences occur so dramatically does go a long way to explain the difficulties that the many clubs in the Football Association have in working together. They are providing very different sorts of facilities, as seen by their supporters. Their supporters are also bringing quite different sets of aspirations and expectations to watching a football match. In any other recreational industry this could be regarded as a great strength. It shows the possibilities of very different markets and of the possible provision of very different types of products. The implied homogeneity of the League and Association of Football Clubs misses a critical recreational and consumer fact of life. The market place is made up of many different groups of people. As in other market places the differences between supporters need to be understood and harnessed rather than ignored.

CULTURE, THE PAST AND PRESENT

So far we have tried to pin down some of the salient differences between clubs which give rise to a recognisably unique culture at each. These differences included such issues as patterns of attendance, patterns of behaviour and attitudes, both towards the club and towards watching football as a pastime. From time to time we have touched upon the background to some of these differences. For example, Celtic was noticeably different to the rest of the clubs on a number of issues, such as attendance and the involvement of political groups. The most obvious reason for these differences is that Celtic was the only Scottish club in the sample. Not only is Scottish culture different from English but the development of football in Scotland has taken a slightly different route, so that there are, for example, differences in the types of crowd disorder experienced in Scotland.[3] However, we can no more consider all Scottish clubs to be the same than we could English clubs. Even within one city, Glasgow, the traditions of its two main clubs are such that they can maintain a deep and long-standing rivalry.

We can go beyond talking about differences between clubs in this specific way to look at what might be described as the culture of a club. While culture is often thought of as an attribute of societies there is a growing interest in organisational or corporate culture. Definitions of organisational culture vary but a good example would be:

> 'a set of common understandings for organising actions and language and other symbolic vehicles for expressing common understandings.'[4]

While this definition was intended to apply to business organisations it can apply just as well to football clubs. A football club is an organisation just as a business is, but with an unusual two-tier structure. On one level there is the professional club, management, players and service staff, who belong to the organisation because it is their job. This part of the organisation may have a very formal structure and the links between members may be based very much on their working relationship. The second level, which consists of the supporters, is more loosely organised. Part of this level consists of the official Supporters' Club, which will have a semi-formal structure, but the organisation also includes casual supporters who turn up to a match if the mood takes them and those people who have 'followed' the team for years without ever going to a match. These people will not know each other and may never meet. Their link is through support for one particular football club.

It may seem rather far-fetched to describe this loose conglomerate of football fans as an organisation. It may seem even more far fetched to suggest that this organisation has an identifiable culture. That the first of these suggestions is in part true has already been demonstrated. Marsh[5] and others identify a 'career' structure for supporters and could even show how a person's spot on the terrace corresponded to his place in that structure. There seems, therefore, to be some informal groupings that members of the football culture can recognise, even if they are invisible to outsiders. Football certainly produces a number of cultural artefacts such as mascots, colours, fanzines, pin-ups and match programmes. But while these artefacts may exist in different forms for all clubs, the difference in attitudes, in 'the way we do things around here', the particular myths and stories of each club, add up to a culture which is subtly unique for each one.

The important consequence of this uniqueness is that cultural differences will extend to the way that the problems now associated with football are realised at each club, to the ways clubs will think appropriate to deal with these problems and to the solutions which best fit with the existing social and physical environment at that club. If we want to do anything about these problems we must answer three questions: What does organisational culture consist of? Where does it come from? Can it be changed?

Craig Lundberg[6], Professor of Management and Organisation at the University of Southern California, proposes four levels of organisational culture: *Artefacts*, which are the tangible aspect of the culture shared by members of an organisation, e.g. stories about past matches or events, rituals, chants, symbols and club regalia; *Perspectives*, the socially shared rules and norms applicable to a given context, e.g. common agreements on appropriate behaviour in a given situation; *Values*, the evaluative basis used to pass judgment on situations, acts, objects and people, e.g. a feeling within a club about what is good football; *Assumptions*, which are the tacit beliefs that members hold about themselves and others, and which form the underpinning for the other three levels, e.g. some may believe that their club is a family club, while others are rough and disorderly.

Where does culture come from?

A large part of the spirit of a club lies in its past: the roll-call of star players and managers, the history of glorious victories and ignominious defeats. Many teams have a traditional arch-rival, quite often a neighbouring team, but usually a well-matched adversary.

Artefacts are the most obviously historical of Lundberg's four levels of culture. The word 'artefact' conjures up images of museums and of archaeological digs. Archaeologists use the physical traces of past civilisations to come to conclusions about their culture. These traces include buildings, such as temples, theatres, stadia and homes, books, paintings and sculptures, cooking utensils and storage jars, jewellery, clothes and toys. Artefacts are equally important to modern football clubs. Indeed the choice of colours, emblems and name are the first acts of a new club. There can even be an attempt to set a tone for the club by a choice of a particular animal as the symbol. A proud rooster or a rampant lion are much more likely choices than chickens or kittens. The team colours can offer a second identification through a nickname such as the Blues or the Lilywhites. Other artefacts, such as stories and myths, grow over time. Some myths are as old as the club but some are only as old as the last match. These can include descriptions of the game, the one perfect goal, a bad refereeing decision, the supporters' day, a witty new chant, an amusing incident that caught everyone's attention, or the clobbering given to rivals.

One of the most important physical symbols of a club is the ground itself. The social history of the club is embedded in and complemented by the grounds. The home turf is the ultimate symbol of a team and the style of the buildings often reflects not only the history of times of success and failure but also the hopes and aspirations of each of those who commission new stands. Because building work is carried out when the team is doing well and revenues are high, the stadium buildings provide an account of the club's life story. A ground like Preston's, which was a showpiece in its day, speaks of a once proud club fallen on hard times. The top clubs of today, like Spurs, can spend money on producing impressive 80s style stands and, the new status symbol, executive boxes. Consequently, some grounds are small and friendly, some merely small. Others are flamboyant monuments to First Division success and modern engineering.

Within the stadium different areas belong to different groups and can have very strong symbolic significances for them. The best-known territories within grounds are the 'ends', the terraces behind the goal-posts, which is traditionally the domain of the young supporters. Some 'ends', for example the Spion Kop at Anfield, have names which are known throughout the football culture. Other territories such as the family enclosure are being developed. This is the only place in the stadium where children have priority. It will be interesting to see whether future generations of football fans see the family enclosure as a symbol of safety and of their first taste of the excitement of going to football.

It is more difficult to speculate about the effect that a club's history and heritage may have on the perspectives, values and assumptions of the club as a whole and on the behaviour of the supporters in particular. Some links are quite straightforward. At one time Liverpool's fans were called the Red Army, both because of their colours and because of the numbers in which they travelled to away matches. They gained a reputation for violence and disruption, which became part of Liverpool's continuing history. A past reputation for mayhem and, from some young men's point of view, good fun, can have two effects on fans' behaviour. First, as we have said before, a club's rough reputation will attract those interested in roughness and repel those who are not, thus changing the balance of opinion among supporters in terms of what is considered acceptable behaviour. Second, the supporters feel that they have a reputation to live up to and may go out of their way to do so. Among adolescents and young people it can be especially important to prove that they are as tough as they believe their peer group to be. That they may base their assessment of their peers on third-hand knowledge, rumours and newspaper reports may only make the situation worse.

Similarly, long-lasting feuds between two teams may build up an expectation of trouble whenever they meet. Each team's supporters may then feel that they should do something about this, either to get in the first move or because the match is on their turf, or because they 'owe one' to their rivals since their last meeting.

On the other hand, clubs which have always been quiet, friendly or sometimes even boring, should have less trouble because these expectations and beliefs are not part of their culture. In this way heritage can be an advantage or a disadvantage to a club, often depending on which aspects of that history are emphasised. In the final chapter we will look more closely at the positive use of club heritage. It does seem that the social rules and expectations for a club may grow from its historical background. This leads us to ask whether they can be changed, or whether they must be left to evolve naturally.

Can culture be changed?

There is some disagreement about whether culture is manipulable. However, there have been successful attempts to change at least some aspects such as attitudes, values and myths.

Lundberg suggests that given the right conditions when the environment both within and external to an organisation is receptive to change, a triggering event may lead to the culture being consciously re-examined. If a rew, preferred culture can be imagined then interventions on all four levels in combination can result in the reformulation of the culture. Without any doubt disasters can contribute to such changes in a dramatic way, although in the period of initial shock this may not be apparent. Other triggering events could be a financial crisis or relegation.

This suggests that culture can best be managed not by trying to thrust a new style on an organisation but by steering in new directions when change is appropriate. If a situation is ripe for change then it can be revised so that aspects formerly taken for granted can be questioned and reformulated.

If culture can be manipulated, then who should be the manipulator? The example of Luton suggests that this can be a task for club management. Indeed, we would argue that it is management's responsibility. Managers must, however, be guided by the mood of the club and be aware of its readiness for change. A lesson can be learnt from Coventry, where Jimmy Hill tried to bring about changes in the face of opposition from the supporters. A change may be intended to move the club forward and to improve the lot of the spectators but may fail because the complex and partly unconscious nature of club culture is ignored.

Managers must also take account of all their club members in the sense that we mean here. Many managers draw a distinction between 'real' supporters and those young men who turn up on a regular basis and then cause trouble. As it appears that these supporters are the most constant and loyal supporters, to dismiss them as not being real supporters at all is facile. If their form of support is not what the management wants, then the management should take some action to change it, rather than disassociating itself from the problem.

CONCLUSIONS

We have shown how the differences between clubs build into a pattern of attitudes and behaviour which characterises each club. We have called this pattern the club's culture. The idea that each club may have its own unique culture suggests that any blanket solutions to football's present predicament may fail because they are not tailored to the situation and the particular difficulties at each club. If we reject single simple solutions, what do we propose to put in their place? Before we can answer this question there are two other important aspects of football to be considered. These are the handling of crowds and emergencies and dealing with violence. The following two chapters cover these, after which we will turn to solutions.

Chapter Four

CROWDS AND EMERGENCIES

THE FRENCH CROWD

Ever since the French sociologists Le Bon and Tarde wrote about rioting of large crowds during the French Revolution,[1] there has been a popular notion that the crowd is a special type of creature. The crowd is seen as something more than a group of individuals: a violent and dangerous creature which must be controlled if it is not to do damage to others or to itself.

Since those revolutionary riots several people have tried to defend the view that large numbers of people gathered together are more likely to behave in a primitive way, responding to events or to leaders in irrational or child-like ways. The individuals who compose the crowd would never behave like this in ordinary day-to-day circumstances. It might be suggested that there is almost a fear of the crowd, or of its worst manifestation – the mob – amongst all people in authority. It must be tamed, restrained and regulated in order that it does not get out of control. Certainly political leaders – particularly in totalitarian regimes – have seen the crowd as an important vehicle for harnessing mass support that might not otherwise be so readily expressed.

It is no accident that when a government is trying to control an unruly population, the first thing it will do is ban any gatherings in public places. As Peter Brook points out,[2] when political censorship is lifted from the written word and from film, it is often still left with the live theatre. Because of the power of dramatic action, live performance before a large number of people is potentially one of the most volatile situations that most societies can create.

Why is it that large numbers of people brought together require careful administration and control, almost independently of the context? What is it in particular that makes the large numbers at football matches require such an intensive system of crowd management, so many regulations and such intensive police activity.

The debate about whether a person in a crowd behaves more irrationally than he or she would on their own, or whether a crowd simply has possibilities for action not available to individuals, has not been resolved. But it is clearly the case that large numbers of people gathered into one place with their objectives and attention focused on a relatively narrow range of events have the potential for doing things that any individual would not normally be able to do. It is helpful to find the reasons for these differences, at a fairly objective level, without being drawn into discussions on irrationality or more exotic notions like that of the 'crowd mind'.

Focus of attention

This heightened awareness of being part of a group with similar interests and commitments is greatly increased by the physical structure of the sports stad'um whereby not only can most people see most other people present but also everybody can see the same central action. There is therefore a focus to attention that can encourage each of the individuals within a crowd to feel a heightened awareness that they share something significant.

This similarity of interest and shared focus of attention may, of course, be concerned with the activity on the field of play in a football match, or it might be with the business of getting out of the ground at the end of a match or in an emergency. As we shall have cause to emphasise later when we explore the problem of emergencies in more detail, the assumption that everyone knows what everybody else is doing is often made but is not always valid. Communications moving from person to person around a crowd take time to be transmitted and can get distorted along the way.

When things go wrong

The excitement of a crowd is, of course, one of its great attractions. One of the great contributions that football makes to our communities is the opportunity it provides for people to be together with large numbers of others enjoying a similar understanding of the skill and drama unfolding before them. Since the days of the gladiators, bringing people together to enjoy sporting activities has always been a recognised part of a civilised society. The problem is that when things go wrong the consequences can be on the same scale as the crowd.

(A) Rare events

If a person stumbles at home they may hurt themselves and even one or two other people who happen to be in their way. If a person stumbles at the bottom of a flight of steps at the end of a football match, when there are hundreds of people coming out of the grounds behind them, the results can be much more serious. One person fell at the exit of a moving walkway at the 1970 Japanese Exhibition causing a pile-up which resulted in 42 injuries.[3]

Rare events have a greater probability of happening in crowds. The more people there are, the more likely it is that one of them may stumble. These incidents have the potential of being magnified into something far more significant because of the sheer density, focus and scale of the numbers of people present.

(B) Weight of numbers

In 1979 some 18,000 rock fans rushed to get through the only two open doors of the Cincinnati Coliseum before a 'Who' concert. Eleven people were asphyxiated in the crush. In the Heysel Stadium 39 football fans were asphyxiated or crushed to death as the crowd tried to escape from approaching Liverpool fans. It is not simply the weight of these crowds in pounds that causes crushes but the communicative and behavioural inertia, which means that once a crowd starts on one course of action it is slow to react to circumstances, partly because of the difficulty of passing information all the way from the site of the danger to the fringes. Typically, those at the back of such a crowd never realise how dangerous conditions have become at the front.

(C) Movement

At all football matches, large numbers of people have to be brought into the ground in the same short period and let out of the ground in an even shorter period. We take for granted the assignment of tickets and the search for different entrances, whether it be to the theatre, bull rings, wrestling matches or football grounds. In many ways the design of all these facilities is really the design of ways into and out of them. They are one vast complex of corridors leading to a circle of seats.

Movement in these corridors must be free and unidirectional. The disaster at Ibrox in 1971 was caused when spectators who had started to leave early from a New Year local derby match turned back at the sound of cheering from the stands. In the crush which resulted between those leaving and those returning, 66 people died and 140 were injured. Steel barriers were bent in the crush, which suggests that a force of at least 4,450 newtons was exerted at that point.

The management of crowds is mainly a problem of the management of the movement of large numbers of people on foot. These people, moreover, are free agents, not drilled to march in step. It is no accident that the first lesson a soldier learns is how to move in unison with his troupe and to follow strict orders directly. This discipline means that soldiers can be moved by foot with superior speed, as they can march as quickly as directed without ever worrying about stepping on the pair of heels in front of them. Football supporters, however, do not march in step getting into or out of a football ground. The design of the grounds and the management of the crowds therefore must in a sensitive way guide and discipline people to enable the movement to be feasible. Given the possibility of those rare events being so significant, as mentioned earlier, the problem of the management of movement can be seen to be even more significant. This problem becomes even more acute during emergencies.

As has been mentioned, some emergencies can be the product of minor rare events that take on a special significance simply because of the large number of people together in a closed space. Other aspects of emergencies can be seen as being more directly a product of the crowd phenomena. A bomb scare, a fight, or a fire, the collapse of a wall, the pressures of large numbers of people in one spot are all very special kinds of problems in places such as football grounds which, although open to the air, are enclosed. They have to be dealt with in rather different ways from the way they would be dealt with in an open field or a private house.

The owner of a private house, or even the manager of a small office building, may be able to live his life effectively without ever considering precisely how any of the emergencies indicated above would be dealt with. This is not true for people who are responsible for the management of football grounds and other large public facilities. The potential calamity of any emergency, however small, is so great that an effective management may hope it will not occur but cannot only think about dealing with the problem if it arises.

THE POLICEMAN'S LOT

How do you know if a football match is going to take place? What are the tell-tale signs that this great event of public interest, sport or entertainment, is about to happen? Anybody who lives within a mile or so radius of a major football ground can tell you immediately. The answer is simply: police.

Hours before the match is due to start, squads of policemen begin to arrive. Streets are closed off. Parking is forbidden. Various pathways that on a normal day would be open to the general public are controlled. As the time for the start of the game draws closer so the number of police and the amount of visible police activity increases.

What is not seen by the ordinary shopper or pedestrian redirected by an unfamiliar young constable, or the local motorist who discovers that he can no longer park where he usually does, is the even larger amount of activity that takes place off the streets and, indeed, on other days of the week. Police forces in areas with large First Division grounds will often have a small team of senior officers who are employed virtually full time on all the preparations and management of football matches. In the London Metropolitan Police area every single member of the police force spends on average two working days a year helping to police football matches. The size of the small army of police inside the football ground can best be appreciated when they fill one section of the stands on being briefed before the match. On one day in March 1985, 4446 policemen were deployed at 40 football matches, an average of 111 per match. The most policed match had 357 officers (Oxford) and the least had 6 (Wrexham). The extent of police presence was not strictly related to the size of the gate, or to the Division, though these factors played some role.

Only 841 of these officers were paid for by the clubs involved. A total of 123 arrests were made, with the highest number for one match coinciding with the largest police presence.

It would be easy to make the mistake of believing that this enormous police activity is simply because of the rowdy criminal element that is being gathered together to watch two groups of grown men kick a leather ball around a field. Whatever the beliefs of the public about the potential violence associated with football this is not the major reason for the police presence. The number of police involved bears some relationship to the number who will be found at other large public events. Political demonstrations, or even the New Year's Eve celebrations in Trafalgar Square, for example, will involve large numbers of police in a circle of half a mile or even a mile radius around the event.

The sheer scale then of a number of people brought together for a football match can, of itself, create a whole variety of requirements for crowd management and control. In Great Britain over the last century we have increasingly assigned responsibility for that control to the police authorities. The public, politicians and the media are so concerned about the potential for disaster and so distressed by any disaster that does occur that a paraphernalia of control mechanisms, from design guidelines onwards, has been created. Let us now consider some of the implications of these processes that bring so many policemen on to our streets around football grounds on a Saturday afternoon.

LEGISLATION BY CRISIS

Given the great public concern and the potential threat provided by large viewing facilities, it is not surprising that a great many controls have developed. The management of these facilities is required to obey a number of laws concerning their design and planning of these facilities. Regular inspections are compulsory and the fire brigades and the police, as well as the local authority safety officers, must approve the physical soundness as well as the emergency procedures before the facilities can be opened to the public. All this control is not surprising and although some may find it irksome few would disagree with the overall value of this type of protection of the public. What does come as a surprise, though, is the way in which the actual guidelines and rules on which this legislation draws have grown up over the years as a result of one crisis after another. Each time there is a major disaster (and they have occurred about every ten years or so this century in football grounds), an inquiry is set up which makes recommendations. There may then be a modification of the rules governing sports facilities. It was only after the disaster at Bolton Wanderers in 1946 that the capacity of grounds, i.e. the maximum number of people who were to be allowed in on any occasion, was specified by law. But these capacities were not enforced throughout football clubs until very much later. It was only after the collapse of the barriers at the Ibrox stadium[4] that legislation was eventually introduced that gave guidelines on the strength of barriers and provided the legal mechanism by which the strengths could be regularly checked, and sub-standard areas of grounds closed. Although the banning of alcohol at football matches was first suggested in reports to the government in the 1930s it was only after the deaths at Heysel that legislation was introduced throughout Great Britain to control the sale of alcohol around football matches.

There is one fundamental difficulty with the process of legislation by crisis: it has all the quality of closing the stable door after the horse has bolted. An accretion of legislation adds in a piecemeal fashion to previous controls. As a consequence there is never any possibility of examining the system of legislation as a whole, of seeing the directions in which it is accumulating or of developing radical solutions that will deal with fundamental problems. A further problem is that rules and principles get built into the legislation in the early years and, provided it cannot be demonstrated that somebody has been injured because of these rules, there is a powerful inertia in the system of controls operating against changing the rules.

A very good example of this is provided by the rules that relate to crowd movement, speeds and widths of passageways. After the Ibrox disaster in 1971 a quick study was commissioned from a firm of consultants, Scicon 40. Their report became the technical appendix to the 1972 *Wheatley Report*.[5]

Scicon themselves say quite categorically in the opening comments of their study that 'until the results are corroborated by further measurements they should be used with caution'. Yet their figures have been built into all subsequent consideration of widths of exit stairways and methods of calculation for the number of people that get out of a sports facility in emergency conditions. Since the early Scicon report there has been some further research looking at crowd movement and especially looking at human behaviour in fires and emergencies. This work throws considerable doubt on some of the figures and principles proposed by Scicon. We shall consider some of these issues in a moment but the important point to realise is that because the *Wheatley Report* figures were enshrined in guidelines and recommendations, no substantial changes have been made in the light of later findings.

From the psychologist's point of view the problem is that there has never been an attempt to develop an organised, theoretically rich account of what actually happens to people in large crowds and emergencies and from this a full understanding of the optimum approach to dealing with these situations. Instead, a set of ground rules has accumulated that is based first of all on police control and second on the addition of ever more sophisticated and solid hardware. Once you decide that it is the police's problem to control individuals and groups in crowds, then it is understandable that the police ask for appropriate laws to be passed to give them more control. Once the laws are introduced it is also natural for the police and others to begin to argue that more police are necessary to help act on these laws and carry out the controls that they are required to operate. In this way an increasing cycle of police involvement is produced that is very difficult to break into.

In a similar way, once it is decided to keep people in small separated spaces and to guide them along enclosed channels to enter and exit from those spaces, then it is natural to hear arguments about making those spaces more protected or effectively segregated. The question as to why the designs need to be handled in this particular way, or whether there is any other way of effectively and safely managing crowds without the need for the hardware of control, can no longer be easily raised. The question becomes increasingly one of how can we get more effective hardware rather than the question of why did we need the hardware in the first place and is there some other way of operating without it. This 'technical fix' as it is sometimes called, whereby the solution to a problem is seen in technical terms and thereafter the problem is defined in such a way that only technical solutions are possible, permeates the engineering approach to crowd safety.

CONFLICT OF INTEREST

The problems of the technical fix and the accretion of legislation without any overall objectives or particular philosophy come to a head when it is suddenly realised that two very different objectives have been aimed at and are now clearly in conflict. This realisation happened most directly as a result of the fire at Bradford City football ground in 1985. While most legislation has been geared to ensuring ready egress from football grounds in an emergency, there has also been a growing desire to try and keep football crowds under control by the increasing use of barriers and other forms of mechanical hardware. When that fatal fire burst out in the stands many people were only able to escape by climbing on to the football pitch. In many other grounds in Britain this would not have been possible because of the barriers that had been erected to keep the spectators from getting on to the pitch. So there was a conflict between the objectives of control and easy egress.

For a time the government inquiry did consider whether some special type of fence could be constructed to solve this problem but, partly because of the advice received from people knowledgeable on crowd behaviour in emergencies, a small step was taken away from yet another technological, hardware solution: it was insisted that the problem lay in giving appropriate information to the crowds and this was a problem of management not of fence design. None the less, segregation of supporters from different football teams and the introduction of ever more electronic surveillance and control systems is still seen as the way forward. These add-on and bolt-to approaches can be handled within the current framework of thinking. They do not require very much more in the way of commitment or understanding from the people who operate the systems. They push the problem back into the concern of the designers and the police rather than the management.

PEDESTRIAN FLOW

One very clear example of the way in which later research has been ignored is the work on the flow of pedestrians out of sports grounds. To understand the significance of the figures involved it should be appreciated that the only basis on which to plan for emergencies at the present time is to consider how long the maximum time should be for people to get from their viewing positions out into a safe location outside the grounds, should there be an emergency. This time is usually given at two and a half minutes for a situation where a fire could develop very rapidly. The calculation then runs something as follows. The narrowest widths along the exit routes are examined and the locations from which people would come to go through these exits are considered. The number of people who could get through these exits in two and a half minutes is then considered and this provides an indication of how many people should be allowed to be in spectator positions that would feed through these exits. This number of people is in effect the maximum capacity that the ground is allowed to hold.

Now, in order to calculate the number of people who could go through the exits the manager, designer, or fire officer needs to have an indication of the rates of flow of the people. The problem is that people do not flow along exit routes like particles of powder or liquids being pumped along pipes. They come in many different shapes and sizes, they're moved by their own unaided efforts and most importantly they move as an undisciplined group intermingling with one another. Such untidiness is, of course, an anathema to an engineer. Many years ago it was therefore decided that people would be considered in terms of a single unit width. This was derived by measurements taken across people's shoulders. It used to be considered to be something like 22 inches but this got metricised to 550 mm. The assumption was then made that people in effect move through doors shoulder to shoulder in discrete chunks of 550 mm each. Somewhere along the line some calculations were also made of the speeds of people moving in free groups on the London Underground and from this a calculation was made in the region of 40–60 persons per minute per unit of exit width. These figures have been enshrined as the flow rates in all regulations and guidelines ever since:

Recommended flow rates
para 233 from stands and stairways a flow rate of 40 persons per minute per unit exit width (i.e. 550 mm) should be used.
para 234 from terraces (including covered terraces) and the ground generally a flow rate of 60 persons per minute per unit exit width should be used.

White Guide,[6] p. 70

Unfortunately, the engineering simplicity of these calculations does not bear psychological examination. A very simple observation would show that people do not move along corridors shoulder to shoulder. The idea therefore that the same number of people would flow out of a doorway that is two unit widths (1,100 mm) as would flow out of a doorway that was, say, two and a half unit widths would seem to be unlikely. Of course, because the guidelines are based on unit widths people normally build in discrete components of this magic unit, so there is not much evidence to show exactly how widths operate. A second point is that people move, quite obviously, at different speeds depending on the density of the crowd. As people get closer together, so it is difficult for them to take larger steps and the shuffling motion that results greatly slows down the speeds at which people actually move. A third complicating factor to which some North American researchers have drawn attention is that people do not normally completely fill exit routes with their shoulders touching walls on either side. Instead they find for a variety of reasons that it is more suitable to keep some distance from the walls, further reducing the effective widths through which they can move.[7]

There is one other very simple flaw in the engineering considerations. The calculation of the use of a set of exits is made by identifying all the exit widths available to people in particular spectating positions and dividing the total number of unit widths by the total number of people. This is an elementary averaging exercise. But anybody who has looked around in a theatre, or at any other public place of entertainment at the end of the performance, will have noticed that unlike engineers' numbers people do not divide themselves evenly between the different exits available. People will tend to go to the exits they know or to the ones that lead in directions that they wish to take.

We carried out a simple study of this process by observing people leaving the stands at Chelsea football ground by one of the main staircases. The stairs had a balustrade down the centre and a separating rail at the top. The crowds using this stairway consistently preferred the right-hand side of the stairs rather than distributing themselves evenly across both sides. There is no evidence that they behave any differently in emergency situations. Furthermore, observations have shown that people tend to join a queue for an exit that seems close, even though another out-of-sight exit may be closer and have no queue waiting to go through it. Indeed this problem of differential egress would seem to be one that would reveal many patterns that have been commented on by behavioural scientists but which engineers have ignored. For example, there would appear to be a tendency to change level first in a complex pedestrian system and then to move along on the final level even when it might be less crowded to move along the first level and then change level at a later stage. There may well also be tendencies to go to the right rather than to the left and so on. Given these problems in calculating and predicting flow rates based on simple engineering principles it is not surprising to discover that researchers in the USA and Canada have actually measured flow rates that are consistently lower than the rates recommended in government regulations.[8]

In principle this might seem to be a potentially disastrous state of affairs. Certainly if the very low figure of 20 people per minute per unit width were contrasted with the maximum assumption in British guidelines of 60 people per minute per unit width then it would suggest that many of our grounds are three times over capacity. The counter to this view is that there is no evidence, even in major emergencies, that the capacities have been inappropriately high. The reasons for this could well be that it is rare these days for grounds to be filled to capacity and we are fortunate that major disasters have never occurred when grounds have been filled to absolute capacity. Even the dreadful happenings in Heysel occurred some time before the match started and before the ground had filled. It is also likely that the two and a half minutes required egress time is much shorter than is essential for many types of emergency. This means that overall the pattern of numbers works out within a safe range. Given this situation, legislative authorities are not very prone to making changes just because the scientific principles and research evidence to support these principles appears to contradict the way they are doing their calculations at present.

However, the consequence of these types of controls, especially when taken together with other considerations to be discussed, is that there is considerable inflexibility in the way in which grounds can be designed. Both the provision of spectator seats or standing positions and the routes into and out of grounds are now so severely controlled by the rigid application of a few key numbers that innovation and variety are very difficult indeed. There is no point in changing the size and shape of doorways, or of introducing a variety of interesting and different spaces along exit routes, when these will all be added together in some very simple calculation of capacity and may well end up indicating that the ground can hold far fewer people than would a conventional design. When the added complications of segregation and other forms of crowd control are put into the picture as well it is understandable that there is so little variety in the way our football grounds are designed for crowd movement.

WHAT HAPPENS IN AN EMERGENCY

Human behaviour in emergencies has been studied by a number of people around the world and it is interesting and valuable to note that their studies do show remarkable consistencies. They indicate that there is a definite set of stages that people go through in all the emergencies that have been studied. What is more important is that these stages do not fit in with the public and much publicised view of wild uncontrolled panic. It is important to establish this difference because many regulations are based upon the assumptions of this notional 'panic'. If something rather different is happening, it may be that once again our regulations derive from a commonly accepted mythology rather from a carefully understood set of psychological processes.

A good example of a situation where this held true was the fire at Bradford City football ground on 11 May 1985. The West Stand, where the fire started, held just over 2,000 people. The stand itself was wooden and had wooden seating at the back, with polypropylene seating on concrete in front of this and concrete terracing nearest to the pitch. Because the stand was built on a natural slope, there was a void under the stand of between 9 and 30 inches. Combustible rubbish, such as sweet papers, cigarette butts and dead matches had accumulated in this space for some time and was probably about 12 inches deep. The fire was most probably started by an accidentally dropped match. The sequence of events which took place was fairly typical for a fire in a public building. The timings are given in Table 4.1.

The first thing to happen is that there are some ambiguous clues that something – possibly life-threatening – may be going on. This

Table 4.1 Sequence of events at Bradford City football ground fire

Minutes	Fire		Brigade/Police and other events	Smoke	Escape
15.40	0 –	Ignition of rubbish	Smell of burning		
15.41	1 –	Serious waste fire – 0.1 MW			
15.42	2 –	Burning of timbers beneath floor			
15.43	3 –	Flames above floor	Call to brigade		Serious local escape
15.44	4 –	Flame above floor (several m²)	TV commences	Serious problems in back corridor	Main escape precipitated
15.45	5 –	Flame under roof (fire at floor level about 10 m²)		Substantial parts of back corridor blocked and lethal	
15.46	6 –	Serious spread under roof and involving roof	Fire Brigade arrives		
15.47	7 –	Stand completely alight			

is an aspect of emergency events such as fires that is frequently misunderstood. In the early stages it is not exactly clear what the nature of the problem may be. All that people know is that there is some possible danger or perhaps only that something unusual is happening. The first sign of trouble at Bradford was when two spectators noticed that their feet and legs were getting warm. They both then looked down and saw the glow of a small fire through gaps in the floor of the stand. This was at 15.40. In these early stages people need to find out what is happening. In a crowd they will ask the people near them or they will listen carefully to any suggestions from figures of authority. The critical point is that some type of initial questioning or search for other information occurs in these early ambiguous stages.

The importance of this early ambiguity cannot be over-emphasised. These quests for further information, checking with each other or looking around, are of critical importance for two particular reasons. First, they take some time to carry out and, second, they lead to a set of expectations as to what is happening and what is the appropriate way of dealing with it.

In the early stages of the Bradford fire it was clear that many people did not take the event very seriously. Spectators close to the fire moved away but then they stood and turned to watch it. In evidence to the Committee of Inquiry, PC Lyes said, 'We did not get much reaction from people in the stand. Obviously they were watching the match and, in fairness, the fire did not look much from where they were sitting. A few of them moved out into the aisles towards the top of the steps.'[9] While one man went to fetch a fire extinguisher, another poured half a cup of coffee on the fire – an action which had no effect. The police were alerted by the spectator searching for a fire extinguisher and they, in turn, went to look before radioing for help.

In the initial stages people in authority may be equally unlikely to treat an incident as serious and so delay taking appropriate action. The police in particular may need time to assess what is going on. In the Bradford fire a senior police officer walked the length of the football pitch in order to examine the fire before he started giving orders for people to leave over the front of the stands on to the football pitch. In Brussels it would appear that the police never got properly organised to deal with the rushing rowdy young men who were chasing around. They appeared to have no clear way of recognising the likely consequences of the actions.

Once some recognition of the early stages has been achieved, people have to start selecting the actions that they will take. This again may require checking with others and will certainly rely upon the knowledge people have of what actions are possible. In certain cases, people may well decide to help others or to go for help.

This then leads on to the third stage in which people actively try to cope with the situation or to leave it. This is when the timing in relation to escape routes, exit widths and the other aspects of egress become critical. It is here that you have a large number of people all trying to leave at once. Their leaving is, of course, under considerable pressure of time, and small accidents can make this into a very dangerous stage.

Because the tempo of a fire increases all the time, the situation can go from being potentially dangerous to extremely dangerous within minutes. In the case of the Bradford fire, there was still time to leave while the flames were growing upwards, but as soon as they hit the roof, the fire could only get oxygen from the open ends of the stand and so spread 'faster than a man can run', sending black smoke ahead of the flames and into the exit passageways behind the stand.

The same time pressure exists in crowd surges and crushes. Pressure can build up slowly but, when critical density is reached, the situation becomes dangerous almost immediately.

It is important to draw attention, however, to the fact that the length of time to evacuate once the decision has been made, is planned to be in the region of no more than two and a half minutes. This is the time it can take any person to get from their position as a spectator out to a safe location. But as has been considered already, the time to recognise that there is something serious going on and then the time to come to a decision as to what to do may be considerable – in the Bradford case, three minutes. Even under normal ideal circumstances, or a situation where the hazard is clearly visible as in the Bradford fire, it can easily take a minute before people decide to act. In more hidden fires, say a fire which originates in a locked room or store cupboard, it can take fifteen or twenty minutes. The importance of these time differences can be assessed by the fact that at Bradford the time from the fire first being barely visible on the television film to its being a total inferno was in the region of from four to five minutes.

It can be seen, therefore, that the early planning for potential accidents, the quick and effective communication and the ready recognition of potential danger and how to cope with it, can all be far more important than having precisely the right number of exits.

Unfortunately, we live in an age in which the technical solution is seen as being more manageable, and possibly of more commercial value than the management or the social science solution. It will therefore come as no surprise that the scientific research which revealed this pattern of behaviour and drew attention to the importance of early recognition and warning has been interpreted to be a reason for developing more complex and sophisticated computer controlled informative fire-warning systems.[10] It is hoped that by producing some clever piece of computing it will be possible to give people information in a way that will greatly speed up their initial reaction and their desire to leave a building in an emergency. In our view, this is introducing just another piece of technology into the chain, with all its likelihood of error and misinterpretation. More importantly, yet again, it inhibits the recognition of where the seat of the problem is: lack of effective management procedures, good training and efficient communication.

WHOSE PROBLEM IS IT?

In this chapter we have looked at the particular problems of crowding and the difficulties that can be caused by emergencies. We have seen that throughout the consideration of the movement of people in large numbers and planning for their safety there has been an increasing tendency to rely on very simple technical calculations built around the idea of the provision of specific architectural means. Where this is not the whole story a disciplined force, in the form of the police, has been drawn on to exert the type of directive control that the steel and concrete cannot achieve.

There has been some change in this mood, that we strongly endorse. This is the move towards recognising that the whole issue is actually one of management and training and the effective communication between various people, football grounds and the public who use them. The more people know about what is being prepared on their behalf, the more active they are in taking part in these preparations, and the more that stewards and club members themselves can do to make this part of their spectator activity, the less likely is it that these preparations for emergencies will ever be called on to be used. A significant consequence of this is that by being part of this overall sharing of responsibilities the physical ambience as well as the social atmosphere of the clubs could well change for the better.

Chapter Five

COPING WITH VIOLENCE

OTHER TIMES AND PLACES

If the British media is to be believed, there seems to be a feeling amongst the public, exacerbated by the Heysel riot, that violence is inextricably linked with football and, in particular, English football. Furthermore, this violence is seen as a phenomenon of the last twenty years. This is a myth. But like most myths, it is firmly lodged within contemporary culture and is extremely difficult to dispel despite numerous attempts by Williams, Dunning and Murphy in *Hooligans Abroad*[1] and Peter Marsh in *Aggro: The Illusion of Violence*.[2] Indeed, in his excellent and highly readable account, *Hooligan: A History of Respectable Fears*,[3] Geoffrey Pearson has shown how long-standing are many of the detailed fears often mistakenly thought of as uniquely characteristic of the present day.

All these and many other writers show that spectator violence is not new, is not particular to football and occurs throughout the world. We shall look at this evidence of the numerous examples of spectator violence in other sports, in other countries and in other times in order to put soccer's problem in context. If football hooliganism is seen to be a recent phenomenon, then it is not surprising that the government and the public believe that immediate solutions of the short, sharp shock kind are practical, desirable and likely to be successful. At present, the problem is seen to be solely a contemporary one and limited to football and therefore amenable to direct and immediate action. But, if it can be understood that football hooliganism is not particular to British culture, that it has occurred as long as football has been played and is not confined to football, then this surely means we must look to explanations and solutions beyond those which emphasise the particularities of today's troublemakers.

Violence associated with sport has been documented since the Roman era. The Romans had two main forms of public sport spectacle, the gladiatorial games and the chariot races. While in the games violence was promoted and sanctioned, inter-competitor violence was prohibited in the chariot races. It was the races, however, which had the highest levels of spectator violence associated with them. Part of the reason for the higher level of rioting may have been that the races were by far the more popular sport. The *circus maximus* in Rome had a capacity of a quarter of a million, far greater than the largest stadium anywhere today. These events were also an occasion for the people to let their rulers know their feelings about the state of the nation. Because the seating was designated according to social class, this gave the rulers an instant public opinion poll as the crowd would shout praise or condemnation for current social policy. So the races were popular, noisy and highly emotionally charged events.

The chariot races were contested by four teams – red, white, green and blue. Over time the first two colours were absorbed by the second two and so most accounts of spectator unrest refer only to the greens and blues. The rioting which occurred among spectators is unparalleled by even the worst violence today and continued into the fifth and sixth centuries in the Byzantine empire. The wooden stadium in Constantinople was burned by crowds in AD 491, 498, 507 and 532. The Emperor Justinian was then forced to build a marble stadium. The crowds did not stop at damage to the stadia. After a green victory in 507, fans ran riot in the city and burned the local synagogue. The greens and blues, dressed outlandishly and frighteningly, roamed the streets and attacked either members of the opposite faction, or innocent passers-by. However, the worst rioting occurred when both factions co-operated in AD 532.

> Prisoners about to be executed were rescued by the mob which ignored Justinian's attempts to appease them with the promise of additional games ... the Emperor acceded to demands that he dismiss John of Cappodicia and other unpopular officials ... the mob proclaimed a new emperor ... and a number of senators paid homage to the new ruler. Fortunately

for Justinian, his most skilful general, Belisarius, arrived in time to save the day – at the cost of an estimated 30,000 deaths.[4]

There are some parallels with football hooliganism. For example, the two factions dressed so that they were immediately recognisable and looked fierce. However, Cameron suggests that the supporters of the blues and greens were *la jeunesse dorée* – well-off young men with a great deal of free time and so possibly rather unlike present-day hooligans, either in England or anywhere else.

Reports of sports-related violence continue from then to the present day. In our introductory chapter we noted the wish to ban football in mediaeval times because it was too violent. In recounting the life of Cromwell, Antonia Fraser[5] reports that in 1655 in the Midlands, football matches and race meetings were banned in order to preserve order. Also from the earliest days of professional football there were difficulties in controlling the crowds. In 1890, at a match between Burnley and Blackburn, the referee was attacked and pursued by a 'howling stone-throwing mob', and the police could not clear the field of supporters. In 1909 at Hampden Park 'some 6,000 spectators pulled up goalposts, fences and pay-boxes, set fire to them and danced round them in the middle of the pitch. Police, firemen and ambulancemen were stoned, fire engines damaged and hoses slashed.' Some 54 constables and 60 other people were injured.

On the day the Popplewell Inquiry's final report was presented to the House of Commons, Mr Toby Jessel, MP for Twickenham, asked whether the Home Secretary, Mr Douglas Hurd, would 'take note of the contrast between the rather better standard of conduct that one might find at a rugby football ground such as Twickenham and the rather lower standard of behaviour at some soccer grounds'.[6] This illustrates quite sincerely the common misconception that soccer has hooligans and other sports have spectators. This is untrue. Even rugby football – noted for its aggression on the pitch – has its share of spectator violence.

Scenes of sports violence are certainly not limited to England. Williams, Dunning and Murphy quote a survey carried out in America which found that 312 riots at sports events (involving 17 deaths) had been reported between 1960 and 1972. The sports involved were: baseball, 97; American football, 66; basketball, 54; ice hockey, 39; boxing, 19; horse racing, 11; motorcycle and car racing, 10; golf, 4; soccer, 3; wrestling, 3; athletics, 2; tennis, 2; and air sports, 2. No definition of what constitutes a riot is given by Williams et al., making it difficult to judge just how severe these incidents were. However, other sources quote details of incidents which give some idea, not only of the amount of damage caused but also of the height of emotion of the crowds.

There was a riot at Roosevelt Raceway in New York in 1963. When officials made what the punters felt was an unfair decision, the spectators stormed the track, attacked the judges' booth, injured one judge, smashed the tote board, broke windows and damaged cars. Fifteen people required hospital treatment. In 1955 a riot occurred outside a stadium where the Montreal Canadians had been playing the Detroit Red Wings. The stadium had been cleared because of disruptive behaviour inside when fans had thrown fruit, galoshes and smoke bombs at a Hockey League official. Outside the stadium fifteen blocks of stores were looted, windows smashed, cars damaged and news-stands and kiosks burned down. Violence has broken out at cricket matches in both Georgetown, British Guyana and Queen's Park, Port of Spain, when bottles and anything else that came to hand were thrown on to the field towards the players.

It sometimes seems that football hooliganism is peculiar to the British. Once again the myth evaporates before the evidence. At a match in Lima in 1964, 318 people were killed in a riot and more than 500 were injured. Seventy-four people died in a football riot in Argentina in 1968, 69 in Moscow in 1982 and 29 in Columbia in the same year. There has been hooliganism in Yugoslavia and in Turkey, where rival fans used pistols, knives and broken bottles. The riot continued for days and 600 spectators were injured and 44 killed. A Dutch player was hurt by a Molotov cocktail in 1981. Some Juventas supporters were armed with flare guns at the Heysel stadium in 1985. Blame is still laid at the door of the English fans who supposedly encouraged violence by their presence or example. Williams et al. describe how English fans were targets for neo-fascist groups in Greece in 1982, who threatened to use pistols and to take hostages if the English fans caused trouble, and reports of hockey hooliganism in Czechoslovakia say that youngsters 'found their idol in Liverpool rowdies'.

The catalogue could roll on. Wherever large groups of people get together there is always some potential for anti-social behaviour.

News reports of major demonstrations almost invariably end, as standard practice, with a comment on the number of arrests or the lack of them.

Where does the origin of football hooliganism lie? Some have suggested that it is the product of individual deviant behaviour. Taken to an extreme, this view proposes that hooligans are innately bad or evil individuals. At the other end of the scale, some sociologists would argue that one needs to look to society to account for hooliganism largely as an outward expression of cultural and subcultural norms and mores. Between these two views, a number of theories has been put forward to explain football hooliganism. In the remainder of this chapter, we will review these theories and discuss the significance of these explanations for developing strategies for dealing with spectator violence. Of course, theorising about hooliganism is not solely an academic pursuit. Those who stand on the terraces are as likely to have theories themselves about soccer violence. It is instructive to consider the full range of possibilities that have been suggested.

WHAT IS FOOTBALL HOOLIGANISM?

Until now, we have been talking about football hooliganism without ever explicitly stating what it is. The kinds of disturbances mentioned range from throwing galoshes to burning buildings. What counts as football hooliganism varies from person to person. It has been found in the past that people often associated hooliganism with vandalism. More recently, there have been incidents of fights and stabbings involving football fans which were counted as football hooliganism even though they took place at some distance from any soccer ground, such as the Embankment tube station in London. Recent violent attacks at cricket matches have even been referred to as 'football' hooliganism!

Although a definition such as anti-social behaviour might seem appropriate, therefore, it would be difficult to be precise about what behaviour is anti-social. More problematic still is defining how much a social problem is *football* hooliganism and how much is, say, rugby hooliganism. Football has suffered from guilt by association.

To some extent incidents are thought of as football hooliganism because of the way those involved are labelled as football supporters. Thus an attack may be considered as hooliganism because the attackers are called 'West Ham supporters' rather than 'regulars of "the Three Stars"', for example. Any of these labels might be equally valid. At a time when football's troubles are newsworthy, attention may be drawn to membership of some groups and not of others. At present, football is seen as a suitable scapegoat.

Definitions of anti-social behaviour can also vary a good deal. It is probably fair to say that most people think of hooliganism as fights, pitch invasions, missile-throwing, drunkenness and the disruption of cross-Channel ferries. Looking at figures for arrests, however, Trivizas found that 67 per cent of arrests were for 'the use of threatening, abusive or insulting words or behaviour, with intent to cause a breach of the peace or whereby a breach of the peace may be occasioned'.[7] These offences generally come under the heading of bawling, shouting, cursing, and swearing and consist of rival supporters shouting sexual jibes at each other with accompanying gestures. Arrests for assaults only amounted to 0.3 per cent of his sample. This disparity between behaviour and arrests stems partly from the difficulties in arresting people in the middle of a crowd. The police are also more likely to charge offenders with offences for which they know they have enough evidence to obtain a conviction. A study in Scotland found that the charges brought varied considerably between police authorities.[8] Even taking all of this into account, incidents of serious violence are relatively rare.

Hooliganism can take place before, during or after the match. Because rival fans are segregated more and more effectively within stadia, face-to-face confrontation is only possible outside the ground. To minimise clashes before and after matches, fans may be segregated both on entering and leaving the ground and in some cases the home supporters are forced to remain inside the ground while away supporters are escorted to their own or the nearest public transport. While one form of hooliganism is thus discouraged, another comes forward to take its place. Fans who are physically separated within the ground can throw missiles, coins or even seats at each other, and Dunning et al. report that 'fighting crews' from some clubs make special forays to find rival fans in places or at times not subject to match-day policing.

Football hooliganism, then, is a term which covers many behaviours, both simple and complex. Although it often refers to the activities of young men found in the vicinity of football stadia on

Saturday afternoons this is too narrow a definition to encompass all that the public associates with the term.

Just as the concept of hooliganism is more complex than it initially appears, then so are the theories put forward to explain why this particular form of aggression occurs and why it should be linked to a popular sport.

Explanations of football hooligans derive from many sources, some treating it like any other kind of aggression involving groups of young men, some concentrating on its attachment to the game itself and to the extent that the two are linked. Some explanations are quite crude and based on public feeling, rumour and media reporting of incidents, whereas some are based on careful examination of what actually happens.

THEY'RE JUST ANIMALS

The most crude explanation for football hooliganism is that hooligans are animals and that the obvious remedy is to lock them up in cages. This explanation is very interesting but tells us more about the people who believe it than about the causes of the problem. For one thing, saying that hooligans are animals is intended to mean in this context that they are sub-human or barbarian and not that they have behaviour or motivations in common with other species, which is an entirely different explanation which we will come to later. The behaviour of hooligans is referred to as bestial and not only in this country. After the Heysel riot, an Italian newspaper carried reports of Liverpool fans urinating on the corpses, reports which were almost certainly untrue but which illustrate how some people believe that soccer fans, once on the rampage, lose all attributes of civilisation and humanity.[9]

By way of a footnote, the term 'animals' was introduced into football by Sir Alf Ramsey. Interestingly, it was applied not to spectators but rather to the players of the Argentinian national side after England had beaten them 1-0 in an ill-tempered 1966 World Cup match in which one Argentinian player was sent off.

Although proffered as a type of explanation, claiming that hooligans are animals is in fact simply an insult referring to the perceived uncivilised, irrational, meaningless violence which many see taking place on the terraces. It also suggests that we – civilised humans – don't need to try to understand what lies behind football hooliganism, or that we could not even if we tried. While a sense of outrage at what is happening to soccer may be justified, it is not of itself constructive. Any real explanation of what football hooliganism is must be based, first, on observation of the phenomenon in question so that we know what soccer violence actually consists of and, second, explanations which can give us some insight into its causes.

'AGGRO' AND THE MALE BOND

Peter Marsh and his colleagues[10] – through studies of the crowds on terraces and detailed analysis of video recordings of incidents of fighting – came to the conclusion that a great deal of what seems incomprehensible and irrational to an uninitiated outsider makes perfect sense and is highly structured when viewed from the point of view of fans 'in the know'.

Marsh et al. put forward the idea (which initially seems rather strange) that football hooliganism doesn't involve violence so much as what they call 'aggro': non-violent ritualised displays of aggression. Their argument is that if observed closely, violence at football matches is more evident than real. Gangs rush at each other but never actually meet. Fans who have seemingly been brutally kicked get up, dust themselves off, and walk away. The violence seems to be of the 'hold me back or I'll kill him' variety. That is, it depends a great deal on looking as if you are willing to do injury, looking hard, carrying knives, but that there are in-built barriers to the occurrence of serious violence – somebody is always there to hold the aggressor back. At worst, a tactical retreat can be effected – i.e., one side runs away.

What is all this aggro for? The suggestion is that aggro is a way of dealing with real aggression, turning it into ritual rather than reality. Marsh et al. say that aggression has always been necessary to man for survival of the species. Man was originally a hunter and aggression was needed to ensure that each tribe or clan had the resources necessary to survive. The existence of all-male hunting groups caused the genesis of male bonding, a sense of attraction and attachment between men in groups. Marsh et al. suggest that this aggression is still part of man's make-up, although they are careful to say that it is not necessary to speculate on whether aggression is inherited biologically. Instead, aggression is so much a part of human culture that it reaches us through socialisation rather than through genes. Another author, Tiger, on the other hand thinks that the propensity for male bonding is genetically linked and that all men inherit it to some degree.

So, aggression is seen as being particularly associated with groups of men. Because hunting was an all-male activity and needed strong co-operative bonds between men to be successful, it is argued that male bonding is now inextricably bound up with aggression. The major difference between men is in how this aggression is made manifest. For most people the aggression is constrained by the rules and expectations of society and it shows up in our culture mainly in competitiveness, so we talk of 'aggressive business tactics'. In any case it is harmful for a culture to allow aggression to be directed towards others without any checks. Much tribal warfare consists of displays of aggression where injury to either side is considered to be a disaster and these 'wars' are seen as one method which primitive cultures have developed to manage aggression.

In the same way Marsh et al. see soccer's 'tribal wars' as one of this culture's ways of allowing men to come to blows without coming to real injury. Young men who are adult enough to be beyond their parents' control, perhaps by being financially independent, without having taken on the responsibilities of raising a family on their own, are temporarily unconstrained. They can show their aggression in more obvious ways than most 'respectable' members of society would choose. Tiger[11] also suggests that young men are particularly aggressive because of their need to seek 'self-validation'. This need for validation, taken with the attachment to male peers, means that proof of maleness is a prerequisite to group membership:

> the combination of the process of attachment and the need for validation leads to a cumulative group 'feeling' which – particularly under the stimulus of external threat or the perception of a possible advantage – tends to increasingly bold and effective activity. The latter characteristic, as much as misinformation, prejudice, inertia, etc., may lead to 'escalation' of conflicts between groups of males for whom conciliation without triumph means invaluation of their maleness – 'honour must be served'.

All of this refers as much to the army, politicians and freemasons as it does to soccer fans. In fact, Tiger suggests that male bonding is a cause of many wars. The difference between the terraces and

Whitehall lies partly in the structures within which this self-validation occurs. Marsh et al. in *The Rules of Disorder* describe a study of the social structure of football fans and describe it in terms of a career structure. Desmond Morris, drawing on the same research for his book *Soccer Tribe*,[12] gives a manwatcher's guide to seventeen identifiable types of soccer fan. The most interesting point about this classification is that it describes a career path from the 'tiddlers', who are just old enough to attend matches on their own, through 'novices', 'fans' and 'leaders' (of chants, aggro or travel arrangements) until graduation as hard-drinking, well-respected, old hands. Within this general structure there are job slots for 'hooligans', 'toughs' and 'nutters'. This 'career path' gives a structure, not only for self-validation but also for the passing on of traditions and changes, for creating an ethos of what is or is not acceptable behaviour. This research, then, portrays young supporters as belonging more to a loosely defined men's club than to a rabble.

TERRITORIALITY

Some theories focus on what are seen as similarities between the behaviour of hooligans and animals. Some animals, robins for instance, have a territory which they will protect from intrusion by other males of the same species. Thus a robin will sometimes attack red objects within its territory, mistaking them for trespassers. It has often been suggested that man is a territorial animal and the fact that soccer fans feel some sort of strong attachment to their 'ends' and try to capture the other side's 'end' if at all possible seems to add weight to this hypothesis. However, the territory fought over at soccer grounds is completely unlike an animal's territory in that it is not valued as a resource for food or mates but as a symbol of the group who 'own' it. According to the Marsh-Morris approach the territories are socially produced as an aid in the aggression-management process. The fact that some violent fans will support their actions by quoting 'territoriality' theories simply serves to show how pervasive social science ideas can become!

While the recognition of claims over ends was made easier by segregation of opposing fans, the division of football grounds into territories can be seen as a way of giving rivals an issue to fight about and an attendant manner of fighting which need not necessarily be violent. In a well-fenced and segregated stadium, small groups of fans may infiltrate the opposing end, disguised as supporters of that side. They can then haul out their own scarves and start to cheer on their team and draw attention to themselves and their feat. On unfenced terracing fans may storm the rival end by force, running towards it in a concerted charge. The two sides may never meet – as the invaders get closer they slow down and a gap is left between the two sides. Some punches may be thrown across the gap but often nothing more serious.

It is obvious, however, that no matter how ritualised the aggression at soccer matches is, real injuries can occur, if not all the time then at least regularly enough to worry both the football world and the public. The 'aggro' theory covers this by saying that if the patterns of the ritual are disrupted by those not involved, for example the police, then the controls which stop aggression tipping over into violence will no longer function. It is argued that by introducing segregation and by moving in to try to stop fights, the police are getting involved in a game without knowing the rules.

A second reason that injury occurs is because even ritualised aggression can be dangerous. When opposing fans rushed at each other in the Heysel Stadium they may not have intended to inflict injury on each other, but the consequences for some of those caught on the sidelines of the action were fatal. Even if we accept the aggro explanation with the proviso that interfering with hooligans can inadvertently increase the level of violence, this theory really says nothing about how to solve the problem. Simply leaving 'the soccer tribes' to fight out their ritualised battles will not remove the possibility of more disasters on the edge of the action.

The theories of male bonding and ritualised aggression make no attempt to explain why so much of male aggression is seen to be centred on football, apart from the fact that, because it is normally supported by large numbers of young men, it provides a good arena for their tribal displays. They are really aimed at accounting for male aggression. A second set of theories focuses more closely on football, its tradition and values and in particular on the changes in these values over the years.

FOOTBALL'S WORKING-CLASS TRADITIONS

Association football is traditionally a game supported by the working class. Originally teams belonged to their locality in a much stronger way than they do now, and the locals who built up these teams and supported them could feel that they were really members of the club. Their support was important and they had a voice in the running of the club. Football heroes were working-class heroes and were presumed at least to hold the same values as their fans. Since the 1930s, however, soccer has turned into big business and although managers will say that what the fans think counts, in fact the directors and shareholders have more influence. While clubs hang on to their local names, their players may not even come from this country, let alone the club home town. The World Cup can seem at times a show case for potential exports! It is not uncommon for players who do well in those games, playing for their country, to move to bigger rewards playing in one of the countries they helped to beat.

Football is a profession and the chance to have a good career both financially and in terms of scope for using their skills becomes more important for players than supporting their home town for the sake of pride. Instead of being a participating member of a local club the supporter is now largely a spectator at a managed event. While Chelsea supporters may regard the Shed as part of their inviolable territory, the stands are not even owned by the club, much less by the supporters. In the summer of 1986, it appeared for a while that Chelsea would be evicted from Stamford Bridge and sent to play at Craven Cottage. Although the move was averted, it is a good example of how far removed a supporter is from the running of the club.

In his analysis of these matters, Taylor[13] pointed out that another effect of soccer changing into big business was that the game itself changed, with more emphasis on defensive play. An exciting, aggressive game gives the spectator more scope for the expression of feelings of excitement, aggression and general arousal. Take this away and, Taylor says, the result is a revolt. The descendants of those working-class men who started the clubs are expressing, in the only way left open to them, their anger at the 'bourgeoisification' of their game. The only other, non-violent, option available is to withdraw support, which would be one explanation for the constantly falling gates.

This argument is taken a stage further by Clarke: he suggests that it is the young fan(atic) rather than the mature spectator who is most alienated from the game, as his attempts to display his emotional attachment and loyalty to the team (such as spraying its name on walls and defending its honour against insults), are rejected by club officialdom. Clarke[14] argues that skinheads were attempting to reassert 'old' working-class values, such as physical hardness, and dressed in a stylised version of working clothes to emphasise this.

THE 'ROUGH' WORKING CLASS

Another explanation which emphasises class differences proposes that part of the reason football hooliganism is so much abhorred is a clash between middle-class attitudes to violence and the attitudes of many football supporters who are members of what has been called the 'rough working class'. Eric Dunning and his colleagues[15] write 'at the risk of simplification our finding is that the majority of football hooligans come from a background where there is a particular conception of masculinity – in terms of ability to fight and loyalty to a narrowly defined community, one where there is extreme male dominance'. This background is what has been referred to as the 'rough' working class, i.e. those at or near the bottom of the social scale. These are the people most often badly hit by recession or depression. Dunning et al. say that men from the rough working class display a particularly aggressive masculine style.

Aggression plays an important role in these men's self-esteem, and young men try to project an image of toughness or hardness by, for example, wearing conspicuously lightweight clothes in winter. Hence the story that 'Millwall fans don't bleed'. Harking back to Marsh and Tiger, Dunning et al. point out that the lower working class cannot gain status and esteem in the ways open to the middle classes, through education and work. Instead they get excitement, meaning and status from 'gambling, street "smartness", and exploitative forms of sex . . . heavy drinking [and] fighting'.[16] This, then, is the sort of bravery seen in cowboy films, where men were men and willing to prove it.

Along with this tough masculinity is a fierce loyalty to community and an antipathy towards any outsiders. The community in question does seem to change, however. In what Paul Harrison referred to as 'the Bedouin effect', people from different housing estates who are 'deadly enemies' all week can be allies on Saturdays in the face of outsiders from another town. Or at a national level, local supporters will bury their mutual antagonism in support of a national team. This loyalty is put at the service of the fan's chosen football club, which will be praised and have its good name defended with chants and, if necessary, with aggression.

SOCIAL BONDING AND VIOLENCE IN SPORT

This is a simplification of quite a complex theory, which claims that attitudes towards violence and its use are tied into the structures of the society we live in. This theory contrasts segmental bonding, where people are linked by ties of kinship and functional proximity, with functional bonding, where relationships are based on work and arise from the division of labour. The length of interdependency chains is seen as being part of the growth of civilisation. While interdependence is based on family groups these chains are kept quite short. Such a segmentally bonded society, held together by commitment to family and locality, is seen as being conducive to physical violence in a number of mutually reinforcing ways.

One important aspect of the society that does not have the extended functional links to hold it together is that the government cannot control the use of violence by the people. The state itself probably has to rely upon the use of force to deal with enemies both without and within but is too weak to claim sole right to the legitimate use of violence, which is therefore more prevalent than is common now. For the mass of the populace work is centred on the local area and there is not a great deal of interaction between different communities. This leads to strong in-group ties, and outsiders, even though they may be ostensibly similar to the in-group, are treated with suspicion. As group attachment is strong, conflict between groups when they do meet is almost inevitable. Each member of a group stands in place of that group, so that an insult to one is felt by all, and may be avenged on any member of the insulting group. The stage is set for vendettas.

Mustafa Sherif and his colleagues[17] would say that all that is needed for this intergroup rivalry is to name two groups and set them in competition against each other, which is what he did in an American boys' summer camp. Other psychologists, such as Henri Tajfel and his colleagues,[18] have produced feelings of in-group solidarity and out-group hostility merely by dividing people into two named groups. Producing conditions conducive to vendettas may, therefore, be as simple as saying 'us' and 'them'.

In a society characterised by segmental bonding, relations within the home are also conducive to physical violence. Work tends to be segregated by sex, so that child-rearing is done by mothers with the fathers absent for relatively long periods of time. Large families and the lack of adequate supervision mean that children spend more time solely in the company of other children. They will then develop hierarchies based on age and strength and may be quick to use violence amongst themselves. Punishment from parents, when it does come, is usually physical, thus legitimating the use of violence. While adolescent girls are encouraged to stay at home, boys are not, and the childhood gangs they have formed may persist into late adolescence and adulthood.

In contrast, a society typified by functional bonding tends to have strong central government which appropriates the use of force to itself and makes its use by the populace illegal. The stability of central government makes the division of labour possible and this in turn makes the structure of the society more complex. Chains of interdependence lengthen, equiring those involved to exercise self-restraint in order that the structure does not collapse. The division of labour also leads to competitiveness because it is based primarily on achievement and allocates status on that basis.

The use of physical violence is forbidden by the state, competition is manifested by the use of foresight and planning towards goal achievement. The injunction against violence is internalised, leading to a greater repugnance for either committing or witnessing acts of violence. Instead of violence being most commonly affective, or associated with emotions, it is now reserved to be used instrumentally, towards some end, such as terrorism.

The social structures are more fluid as people move from area to area following their work rather than their extended family. There is equality of the sexes and more supervision of children, who are discouraged from the use of violence and are given fewer examples of its use by adults.

Dunning et al. suggest that our society has been changing from segmental to functional bonding. Changes of this nature occur more or less from the top down in a society, so while most of today's society leans towards functional bonding, the rough working class, at the bottom of the heap, are still struggling with segmental bonding.

Therefore, the reason that football hooliganism is so abhorrent to society is not that it is new, or that the violence is a marked increase on the levels of violence in the past, but that the majority of society is simply less tolerant of these displays of aggression.

PLANNING AND POLITICS

Thus far we have seen that soccer hooliganism can be seen as a way for young men to manage their inherent aggression, which is consistent with the values of their class and which may be a form of protest from a disenfranchised section of society. As such the problem is at least understandable and at best can be dealt with, even if not through short-term solutions. There have, however, been developments on the football scene which call into question the relevance of these theories for the hooligans of today.

There is mounting evidence that hooliganism is no longer a spontaneous expression of emotion or even of pent-up aggression but a purposeful activity, planned in advance. The planning is said to be done either by extreme right-wing political parties who want to gain supporters and to destabilise society, or by groups of hooligans themselves who organise small armies and plan their engagements in advance. If it is true that the aggressive climate at matches is being manipulated or at least taken advantage of, then this is more worrying in the long term than relatively disorganised crowd disturbances.

The influence of political groups

There is a widely accepted idea that extreme right-wing parties have a strong influence on terrace violence and some would go so far as to claim that violence is instigated by cells among supporters. The evidence for these views comes from a variety of sources. Racist chanting and Nazi salutes are common enough on the terraces. Black players are booed, even by their own team's supporters.

There was some evidence that members of extreme right-wing parties were at the Heysel stadium in Brussels. The Mayor of Brussels saw both English and Italian fans wearing insignia of such parties. The ground outside the stadium was reported to have been littered with their literature.

However, there was no hard evidence that extreme right-wing parties caused any of the violence.[19] It seems most likely that, while these groups may be popular among some groups of supporters, they cash in on violence rather than being its instigators.

There is a danger that the effects of racism and the influence of political groups may be confused. It is often assumed that those who support extreme political parties of either right or left are aware of and agree with most, if not all, of their chosen parties' policies. In fact, Billig and Cochrane, in a study of fifth formers, found that supporters of fascist parties knew very little about their policies and often could not recognise any of their leaders. They supported these parties simply because they advocated the expulsion of non-whites from Great Britain. Billig and Cochrane[20] call this phenomenon 'symbolic politics' because the appeal of such parties to these school students was a symbol of racism. Now, according to Williams et al. the typical football hooligan is given to xenophobia and views with suspicion anyone who does not come from his own community. From this point of view, racism is simply an extension of this attitude to those who 'don't come from this country' even though they may have been born here. By this reasoning football hooligans may be likely to support extreme political parties. It does not mean, however, that such parties control the actions of football hooligans.

To search for further evidence on this important matter we asked those in our survey the question, 'Do you think that organised political groups are involved?' but this percentage varied from 11 per cent at Sunderland to 65 per cent at Chelsea. The party most often mentioned was the National Front, or other extreme right-wing groups, but in Glasgow the IRA was also mentioned. If interviewees thought that there was political involvement they were then questioned about the reasons for their belief. What we wanted to find out was whether anyone had any evidence based on first-hand experience. 162 respondents said that they had such direct evidence. It transpired that some of those people had 'seen' this evidence in the media. The interview went on to ask what members of groups had actually been seen to be doing. It seems that the most common activity was distributing literature, with very few instances of involvement in fighting.

So, although quite a number of people believe that political groups are involved in football hooliganism, this belief must be based mostly on hearsay and media reports. In some clubs, such as Sunderland where only 1 person out of 100 had seen such a group member fighting, we can safely conclude that political involvement is not an issue.

All this does not, of course, rule out the possibility that hooliganism is in some way organised, even if not by political groups. There is some evidence that the nature of hooligans and hooliganism is changing. But the view that they are now organised groups of youths, with identifiable leaders and specific objectives, is certainly not new. Pearson, for example, points out that throughout the last century and before there was a constant stream of complaints about hooligan leaders and the way these organised groups were wreaking havoc. Certainly it is true today, as we have learnt from discussions we had with the police that fans may sometimes be ambushed away from the grounds. This implies that attacks are not impetuous 'heat of the moment' affairs, but premeditated actions planned with an almost military-style strategy.

THE 'NEW' HOOLIGAN

Mr Justice Popplewell, in his final report, made particular mention of a certain type of troublemaker, the 'new' hooligan. While the popular image of football hooligans was still of tough, badly-dressed yobbos or skinheads, football fans and the hooligans among them had been developing a more sophisticated style, both in their clothes and in their warfare. And warfare it seemed to have become. Leslie Muranyi, a Cambridge supporter who was sentenced to five years for leading attacks on visiting Chelsea fans, was nicknamed 'the General' and his followers were called soldiers, at least by the press. Furthermore, the main attack on the Chelsea supporters involved them being trapped by a pincer movement so that they had no escape. It certainly seemed that hooliganism was not limited to unorganised charges on the terraces.

There are several interesting differences between the 'new' hooligan and the rough working-class type. The first is the obvious presence of money. Steve Redhead and Eugene McLaughlin[21] in an article entitled 'Soccer's Style Wars', chart the progression of fans' style from Fred Perry T-shirts to Armani jumpers. The clothes must not only look good, they must also be obviously expensive. In the same way, fans buy tickets for seats and then jump up and down waving at the less conspicuously wealthy friends on the terraces. Southerners taunt Northerners about their poverty and Merseyside seems to be taunted by everyone. Redhead and McLaughlin say, for example, that 'London casuals have flashed £5 and £10 notes in the same manner as the Metropolitan police did on the Yorkshire coalfield during the Miners' strike' and sing,

> 'Sign on, sign on with a hope in your heart
> and you'll never get a job'

or

> 'One job between you,
> You've only got one job between you'

Further, these fans are willing to spend money to escape the attentions of the police. For example, having season tickets means that they don't have to stand in queues outside the ground, where the police have a good chance to look them over. However, the best-known tactic is the use of normal bus and train services to go to away matches, rather than 'football specials'. Some of the most famous 'fighting crews' are named after their use of public transport – West Ham's 'Inter-City Firm', for example. (The fighting crew is a more or less loosely defined group of fans who come together before matches simply to plan aggro.) So these new hooligans travel in comfort and anonymity, sometimes first class, and arrive refreshed and certainly not drunk. Nor does their ingenuity stop there. The Portsmouth '6.57 crew' travelled unchecked to Cardiff by hiring morning suits and pretending that they were going to a wedding.

Another interesting difference is that there is some evidence that the leaders of the gangs are in their mid- to late twenties and, recent arrests show, some of them have relatively skilled jobs, such as solicitors' clerks. Gang warfare and displays of aggression in general are usually associated with younger men or even adolescents, the idea being that as they grow older they grow more mature and take on social responsibilities which tie them more into 'acceptable' society. Marsh et al. for example, identified a group who were respected by younger fans for their hardness and past deeds but who did not take part in the aggro themselves.

Taken together, these differences suggest that the 'new' hooligan is not just the 'old' hooligan dressed up: an entirely different type of person may be getting involved in football violence and possibly for entirely different reasons. Why should they want to? Terrence Morris[22] suggests that being involved in a fighting crew, particularly in the leadership of it, is an opportunity for the kind of recognition and status that is difficult or even impossible to come by in a normal working life.

Although there is some evidence for the 'superhooligan', it is not completely convincing as a general explanation. First, although much is made of the wealth and supposed middle-class origins of these new hooligans, Leslie Muranyi was a window cleaner and others arrested have not had highly-skilled or professional jobs. People should not need reminding that you can look neat and well-dressed without being middle class. Even if they cannot save or borrow the money, youngsters with criminal tendencies can get expensive 'casual' gear by what is known as 'taxing' those young enough to be intimidated. Taxing simply means taking a buyer's purchases as he leaves a shop. Girlfriends can often be persuaded to turn hard-earned cash into Pringle sweaters as proof of true love. Second, just because someone is nicknamed 'the General' does not necessarily mean that he leads an army. There is little hard evidence that fighting crews are organised to the extent that one might expect from labels like army. It is also important to recognise what might be termed the 'psychological benefit' of any explanation. For instance, being able to dismiss hooliganism as the work of a few determined criminals allows clubs to define the problem as one which the police must solve. Suggesting it is endemic to a whole approach to football is much more threatening to club management.

The strongest test of any theory is whether it allows us to make predictions about the phenomenon in question. So, while explanations of football hooliganism have an intrinsic curiosity value, their only practical value is that they may give clues as to how hooliganism can be coped with or discouraged. On the other hand, all the measures taken so far to deal with the problem are based on theories, whether or not these are ever made explicit. Attempts at coping with hooliganism can be grouped loosely under two headings, prevention and cure. 'Prevention' refers to attempts to prevent or contain violence in the short term, and 'cure' to more radical attempts to change the nature either of football or of the hooligans themselves.

PREVENTION

Theories of hooliganism as purely barbaric, anti-social behaviour lead to the use of strong-arm tactics by way of prevention – for instance, physical segregation and heavy policing. The idea is that rival fans cannot fight if they cannot get at each other, so fences are erected around the pitch and across terraces. Where physical barriers do not exist the police are used to form human barriers. This is only a stop-gap solution to the problem. Every preventative measure can be combated by the hooligans. Missile-throwing takes the place of face-to-face confrontation, segregation within the ground displaces the aggression to outside the ground, a police presence forces anyone looking for trouble to plan ahead. Therefore the symptoms change but the illness remains the same. These preventative measures can also have unexpected side-effects. Marsh et al. discuss how segregation gives sides a much more recognisable territory to defend and has facilitated the emergence of the 'ends' as physical symbols of the club's honour.

A more sophisticated measure is the issuing of membership cards which can be withdrawn if the holder transgresses. The underlying assumption here is that there are identifiable trouble makers at work and that if they could be excluded normal, decent fans would be free to carry on watching the game in peace. The introduction of closed circuit television is encouraged on the same basis. But whatever is said about the existence of 'superhooligans' or of gangs with obvious leaders, Dunning et al. would dispute the idea of hooliganism as being instigated by a few ringleaders, as they see the roots of hooliganism as being buried in the inequalities of the social system.

CURE

Attempts at a cure have taken a shorter or longer perspective. Like preventative measures they can take either a physical or a more social form. Under the heading of physical would come the all-seater stadium. It is well known that trouble usually flares up on the terraces while the seated areas are quieter and safer. There seemed to be two reasons for this. First, the differences in physical layout means that individuals remain individual in seats as supporters cannot bunch up as on the terraces; furthermore, crowd movement is cut down to a minimum. These factors make a seated crowd potentially more manageable. Second, attitudes are different for those who sit, as shown by our survey results in Chapter 2. Therefore more seats, combined perhaps with a discriminating pricing policy, should encourage more respectable supporters, particularly women and families, and discourage the less respectable.

When Coventry created their all-seater stadium, it was this second assumption which alienated their supporters. People who had previously watched from the terraces felt that they had been branded as hooligans by the club and naturally resented this. The Coventry experiment went down in history as a failure but this judgment is unjust because as an experiment it did have some interesting findings. We will return to the question of all-seater stadia in Chapter 6.

A similar initiative is the introduction of family enclosures. Again, the physical environment is being altered with a view to attracting a more 'peaceful class' of supporter, but at least in this case families can be encouraged without others feeling insulted. Family enclosures are not designed to keep families in, as the name might suggest, but to keep the rougher elements of the crowd out so that some level of safety can be guaranteed for families in the match ground. As mentioned in Chapter 2 we asked the clubs whose supporters took part in the survey whether they had made improvements since that time. Manchester United, Sunderland and Millwall replied and all had introduced family enclosures. Sunderland had also started a club for younger club members called the 'Roker Rookies'. This initiative is an obvious next step from promoting soccer as a family entertainment and could lead into stronger community links, a topic also taken up in Chapter 6.

CONCLUSION

Nobody can offer a complete explanation of football hooliganism nor a magic solution. What is most striking about the theories discussed here is that they all seem to have some truth for some aspects of the problem. The psychological theory of Marsh et al. suggests that what we are concerned with is an essentially non-violent, rule-bound ritual now warped by external pressures into bloody battles. The more recent sociological theorists concentrate on the stratum of society from which the core of football hooliganism is drawn. While they reject the Marsh theory, partly because of the obvious violence in hooliganism today, their theory is based on the idea that a sub-culture exists – 'the rough working class' – that has different rules for guiding their behaviour than does the rest of society. By taking the Dunning idea that one section of society has a different structure and therefore different values and priorities from the rest, we can explain why some young men do their bonding in politics, men's clubs or the army, while some do it on the terraces. Thus, the two theories do complement each other quite well.

Both theories, however, have problems of their own. First, it is now difficult to distinguish between acts of violence and disrupted ritual aggression. If someone has a broken glass thrust in his face it is simpler to explain this as a violent act than as an aggressive act where the constraints placed on the violent display of aggression have broken down. This does not necessarily mean that the theory does not hold true, but that it is almost impossible to imagine a situation where it could be disproven, usually a bad sign in any theory.

Second, Dunning et al. say that not all hooligans are from the rough working class, nor do they all come from specific areas that have closely-knit communities. We are therefore left without any explanation as to why these others turn to football hooliganism. Are they simply attracted to the violence or do they want to be involved in some aspects of its camaraderie?

Third, neither theory can explain why football became the focus of this aggression. Marsh et al. consider football as only one possible arena for aggro and do not seem to feel that it offers anything that any one of a number of other arenas has not offered in the past or will not offer in the future. Dunning et al. see the football club as an extension of the local community, as a symbol of the locality. There are other working-class traditional pastimes that do not attract the same protective interest.

Finally, neither theory offers any implementable solution to the problem. Now it is true that there are not always simple solutions to every problem and that football has suffered from having 'easy' solutions foisted on it. It seems though that if we attempt to explain what causes football hooliganism or to describe what it actually is, we should be in a better position to say how or whether it can be stopped. The solutions need not be short term, or even medium term, and they need not be simple or neat, but they should be there.

FOOTBALL IN ITS PLACE

Marsh et al. simply suggest that the problem will eventually go away of its own accord, that young men will move their arena of conflict on to a different site, thus giving us the same problems in a different context. Dunning et al. in a more constructive but, given the state of the world, less hopeful vein, suggest that the ultimate solution is a more egalitarian society.

Having said this, we must ourselves offer some ideas for a way forward. We will do this in Chapter 6. These suggestions will be based on three perspectives:

(1) that football hooliganism is only one of football's problems,
(2) that the environment which is its focus plays a role,
(3) that there cannot be one solution for all clubs.

Chapter 6

THE FINAL SCORE

Being present in the stands or on the terraces is often described as enabling a person to feel the 'atmosphere'. This includes the experience of being in a crowd, being able to feel that you can encourage your team on the field by your proximity. It enables you to be aware of the weather and other local factors that cannot be readily gleaned from some secondhand account; to see all the action and the crowd response to it. Furthermore, to have 'been there' is a reason for going.

If 'being there' were not a crucial factor, there would not be the scramble for FA Cup Final tickets each year. Tickets are sold perhaps at ten times their face value even though the match can be seen live on television. It bears no comparison with being seated at home, where you cannot taste the moment. You cannot feel at one with so many others, appreciating the skill and strategy on the bright green turf, holding your breath with thousands of others or cheering on the players as their moves succeed.

What is being described here is the experience that derives from visiting a place of entertainment. It is surprisingly rare for football grounds to be discussed in these terms so there is really very little information about how successful football grounds actually are as recreation or entertainment facilities. The investigations that we undertook and reported earlier did look at this directly but there is only a handful of other studies with which we could compare our results. We believe that it is essential to think of the recreational experience of football grounds because the experience we have described may be destroyed by the way grounds are designed, managed and policed.

There remains little direct examination of football as part of the entertainment industry. A few British football clubs have attempted to examine their activities like effective commercial enterprises, including commissioning market research studies, but as far as we can find out these studies have rarely been acted on or taken seriously as part of a long-term plan. Theatres, cinemas, hospitals, shopping centres, schools, offices, hotels, museums and even prisons have all been studied in order to take account of the experiences of the people who actually use and manage those facilities in their administration and design. This book has sought to do the same for football grounds.

Such studies are often referred to as studies in 'environmental psychology'. The 'environment' studied is the physical, architectural, urban and natural environment – those aspects of the inanimate world that are shaped to human ends. The 'psychology' comes from the systematic, scientific study of human transactions with that environment. For example, psychologists have explored the ways in which prisons can be designed to produce less destructive places of incarceration; psychologists have been involved in managing and planning national parks and forests in order to ensure that people can enjoy and understand them without destroying them.[1] Banks have been redesigned on the basis of psychological research, trying to see the bank layout as criminals would, thereby reducing the feasibility of a successful raid and ensuring, for instance, that the important lines of sight and clear escape routes a robber would use are not provided. The stresses people suffer that are associated with aircraft and traffic noise have been extensively examined by psychologists as has the impact on a community of the introduction of a major new road through its midst.

These studies use a great variety of methods and draw upon many different types of psychological theory. They have been carried out all over the world. We have tried to begin to apply this type of thinking to the management of football and the design of the stadia it uses.

THE PROBLEM

The special quality of football and the place in which it occurs would be of little public interest if it were not for the fact that, for a number of years now, football and the places that make it a professional sport have been under threat so much so that the media have sometimes referred to this as a problem of 'crisis' proportions. Any serious consideration of our national game suggests that if there are not radical changes it will soon slip into a minority spectator sport.

The problem is captured very directly in the falling attendances at football matches. In the early 1960s around 30 million attendances were recorded at English Football League matches each year. Twenty years later attendances were less than 20 million. A simple extrapolation of these figures demonstrates that by the turn of the century football may well have ceased to be a spectator sport in the UK. The simplicity of the calculation hides the fact that the decrease in the last ten years has been much more rapid than the decrease in earlier years, indicating that the demise could be sooner rather than later.

Direct appeals to the competition from television or the general decline in active participation in sports is not borne out by the facts. In the main the decrease in attendance at football continued after television was widely and well-established in British homes. The evidence that can be gleaned is that showing football on television actually increases the number of those who wish to see it 'for real', as is the case for many other television activities. While, for example, attendances at football matches have declined, attendances at tennis matches, notably Wimbledon, or at major snooker tournaments, have continued to grow. It would seem that this is because of, rather than in spite of, television coverage. The Lords test match can attract nearly 100,000 people (over five days) and Wimbledon more than 400,000 (over its fortnight).

Certainly the figures on recreational participation, from dramatic societies to aerobics and mountaineering, do not indicate a population that is settling unthinkingly into its armchairs in front of the television. In the General Household Survey nearly half of those questioned had actively taken part in some sport in the previous month. Even the cinema and theatre have been able to fight back, to some extent, against the more direct inroads of television. In a country where more and more people have more leisure time the one industry that is consistently growing is the recreation and leisure industry. Yet against this background football is consistently losing its attraction.

Despite the fact that attendances at football matches have been falling over the years, the game of football is still one of the regular situations in which a very large number of people are brought together. Figures ranging from 20,000 to 50,000 are still not uncommon for weekly First Division football games. So football has some particular interest because of the consequences of the large crowds that exist there.

As we discussed in Chapter 4, since the latter part of the nineteenth century there has been consideration of the particular properties of crowds. A number of social scientists have argued that crowds are a rule and law unto themselves whereby people behave very differently simply by virtue of being with many thousands of other people. Whether this is true or not, it is not part of our normal experience to be together with so many other people.

The focus that requires everybody to be able to see all aspects of the game gives rise to a design in which large numbers of people have to be channelled into particular locations at which they can either sit or stand to watch the game. There is a build-up and concentration of people, and at the end of a game a dispersal, which gives the stands and terraces a part to play in the overall experience of the crowd that is not present in many other large gatherings. There is a very real sense, therefore, in which the stadium itself is part of the experience of the crowd in that it encloses the crowd in a particular area with its own very special orientation.

The contrast with a race meeting or golf championship is helpful. Although the crowd sizes may be very big at these gatherings (more than 140,000, for example, at the British Open Golf Championship) the concentration of the crowd in one particular enclosed space is not as great as is the case at football grounds. This means that the movement of people in and out of the golf course and their distribution around it is a much more relaxed and long-term experience, far less tied to the particularities of the architectural structure than is the case with a football ground.

MECHANICS OF CONTROL

Over the last few years the experience of a football match has also been strongly influenced by a variety of control processes. In Britain, at least, supporters of different teams are separated and assigned to different parts of the ground. Movement around the ground during a match is severely restricted. The presence of the local police force is very apparent. Indeed, many police forces have a senior officer who is employed virtually full time in order to prepare for and supervise the regularly occurring football matches in the district. As is apparent from an examination of any major incident at a football match, it is the actions of the police that are the dominant influences on how the incident is managed. The police are, of course, responsible for crowd control in many other circumstances, but at the football match their influence is virtually total. They will give instructions as to when gates ought to be opened or closed, when matches ought to be cancelled or postponed and will try to have an influence on the way in which tickets are bought and sold. Increasingly sophisticated police intelligence is also focused on football supporters and football matches. The recent arrest and charging of a number of people believed to be planning major disturbances at football matches was the result of intensive police intelligence work targeted directly at football supporters. Bomb scares and other threats now associated with airport terminals and other major public gatherings are not unknown at football matches as well.

The present attempts to manage the problems football currently faces are difficult for those outside the game to appreciate. As many as 55,000 police days were probably accounted for in London last season at football matches. The number of police typically involved in any major game runs into the hundreds. The friendly spirit of sporting competition, supposedly as a way of harnessing minor rivalries to support a game of skill, is accompanied by police escorts and ground segregation that would do justice to a military manoeuvre. Police preparation for any given match begins days in advance, starts with great intensity hours before a match and often finishes hours later. The football authorities, supporters and politicians alike see this police involvement as necessary and inevitable.

Every government report on football crowds this century has added to the police burden and increased their powers. One major consequence of this is that the problems of violence, and the other less frequent hazards and discomforts associated with football, tend to be seen as a problem in policing. Two approaches or models have been followed with regard to recognising and dealing with football's 'off the field' problems. The first strategy is that of denial. A parallel can be drawn here with the behaviour of mental patients, whereby a painful and difficult problem is dealt with by denying its existence. The second strategy is 'displacement', whereby attention focuses on either the symptom or on another part of the system. It is hoped that by tinkering with the symptoms or suggesting that it is someone else's problem, the 'illness' will either go away or can be ignored by those who have direct responsibility for finding a cure.

We are not denying that there are quasi-criminal, rival gangs that cause chaos from time to time in our cities. Knowledge of such fights between factions can be traced back at least as far as the tragic confrontations between Shakespeare's Montagues and Capulets. Although the same groups may or may not be involved within the stadia as outside, there is a difference between violence and aggression within a privately-owned place of entertainment and gang fights in the streets. The police are rightly involved in all attempts at the control of these incidents in public places.

One of the causes of this state of affairs has been what is sometimes referred to as 'legislation by disaster'. Instead of keeping a watching brief on the state of British football, successive governments have waited until some major incident has occurred. They have then introduced controls that would have limited that disaster if they had been in place before the disaster occurred. The most recent disaster in Bradford has already given rise to a new Act of Parliament covering 'Fire and Safety at Places of Sport'. This will mean that any covered stand that seats more than 500 people will require a certificate from the local authority before it can be used.

Legislation by disaster ghoulishly waits for some other disaster to occur in some other way for that particular problem to be dealt with. One sign of this approach to legislation has been the series of official reports throughout this century. Virtually every decade there has been a major government inquiry into some aspect of football. These reports make fascinating reading not least because of the way in which the same themes are picked up by the reporting groups again and again along the way. For example, the recently introduced legislation that bans alcohol at football grounds and on the coaches and trains that carry people to football matches and which is now hailed by the Home Secretary as such a strong contribution to the reduction in crowd violence, was first recommended in an official report at least thirty years ago. It was mentioned in two subsequent government reports before it was eventually acted upon.

No other sport has generated such debate and legislation, or is calling out so clearly for a radical change in its approach to its supporters. What is it, then, that makes football so special? The answer lies in the fact that besides the problems that football faces, it also brings together a unique combination of factors. For although football crowds, football stadia, football violence, football disasters, the excitement of football, the pleasure and despair of watching football all share much with other events and incidents, the combination of them all *together* is rare. A crowd watching a pop concert may be as large, if not larger, than a crowd watching a football match. The excitement which an audience feels from a speech by Billy Graham may be similar to the excitement that the home crowd feels when Everton scores. The violence of a gang of teenagers fighting in the streets with another gang is just as distasteful and horrifying whether the gangs are wearing football supporter scarves or Hell's Angels jackets. The problems of crowd control for people going to Wembley Stadium for a Cup Final are very similar to the problems of people going to the same stadium for a rock concert, or people going to Trafalgar Square for a peace campaign demonstration. But people only associate *all* these different activities and experiences with one event: football. Football, then, brings together an intriguing combination of special circumstances.

WASTED ASSETS

Another aspect of this problem is the fact that a major investment in the form of football grounds themselves is no longer being utilised to the extent that it could within our towns and cities. These large holes in the urban fabric could supply sorely-needed venues for a great range of public activities. Therefore, as a community resource they are under-utilised. Clubs like Arsenal have developed training facilities such as the Sobell Centre, which is available to the local community when not required by the club. But in general, football stadia comprise several acres of ironwork, concrete and grass used for an average of one or two matches a week. At many matches the terraces are only half full. Reserve matches of First Division clubs may attract less than 1,000 spectators. For the rest of the week the terraces are empty and the pitch only occasionally used for training. Surely, in any other situation, the company accountant would be horrified that so much investment was tied up in a capital asset that was used so little and gave such a limited return. This situation suggests that grounds should be used more effectively so that they are in productive use for more than just a few hours a week.

Most industrialists who require 'plant' for a limited time would hire it rather than own it. Given this argument, it would make more sense for football grounds to become community assets owned by local authorities, a local trust, or private entrepreneurs with wider interests than just football. By these means they would become community assets in a psychological, social and economic sense. In this way, grounds could be brought up to the sort of standard expected of entertainment facilities in the 1980s.

OWNING THE PROBLEM

Consider the world of popular music, that attracts to a certain extent a similar age range and social mix to that of football. If a pop group attracted fans that destroyed a concert hall, as has happened, then the pop group would not be invited back again to that hall. Indeed, they might not be invited to play anywhere else! In the case of football, the problem is somewhat different. Football clubs are limited liability companies, which are businesses as much as objects of reverence. Clubs have little control over who gives them support. While they can refuse entry into the stadium, they have no control over their 'supporters' when on the streets. The problem is exacerbated by the fact that the clubs cannot stop them wearing the colours of the football team and thereby inducing an immediate association between their behaviour and the club. Again, we have the phenomenon of guilt by association. On these grounds it seems absurd that the footballing authorities such as FIFA can hold a British club responsible for the actions not of its employees but of people who have no formal relationship with the club at all. Such supporters do not represent the club, either *de jure* or *de facto*. Therefore it is difficult to understand how the club can be held responsible for their actions.

What football clubs can be held responsible for, though, is a failure to instil any sense of belonging, identification, and a sense of responsibility towards the club. They should be encouraging their supporters to believe that they do represent the club and are their ambassadors.

This identification already exists in embryo. One only has to listen to the conversation of any group of football supporters and as a matter of course they will talk about 'we' – 'We won the match', 'We won the semi-final of the Cup' or 'We were awful.' For some supporters though, it has got to be made more real than apparent. More than 150 years ago Jean-Jacques Rousseau and John Stuart Mill wrote about the importance of participation in public affairs, the community benefits of such participation and the need to educate people to participate effectively.[2] If there was more participation in football's affairs, and supporters were educated to participate, then this sense of belonging and responsibility might well develop as Rousseau and Mill suggest.

The problems associated with football and its urban location have not emerged suddenly. Because of the extent to which it is in the public eye and the large numbers of people who have been associated with it in the past, major incidents at football grounds have always been worthy of public note. Throughout this century there has been a cumulative series of highly publicised events that have added to the disquiet now expressed with the state of British football.

The earliest incidents were partly a function of the lack of experience in controlling very large crowds. In 1923, crowd disorder occurred at the first ever Cup Final at Wembley Stadium. This and later disasters, such as that at Bolton Wanderers when a barrier collapsed and 33 people were killed, were caused partly by too many people being crammed into too small a space. Such densities are no longer possible because of the controls that have long since been introduced. However, much of the experience and collective memory of football matches still draws on the sheer density and crush that is associated with large numbers of excited people in an enclosed space. The 'White horse' incident at Wembley Stadium captured in the famous photograph of the 1923 Cup Final when a policeman on a white horse kept the crowds from spilling on to the pitch is part of the mythology of football.

One of us recalls regularly attending a Third Division football ground where spectators arrived at the ground fairly early so they could lean against the crush barriers to watch the match. This single piece of terrace furniture was the one minor concession to spectator comfort. Of course, it was realised that its real purpose was to stop crowds tumbling down the terrace. What was not appreciated on going to Anfield for the first time was that its function was that of protection for those in front of the barrier rather than comfort to those leaning against it behind. And so the first Liverpool attack on the Kop end, when the crowd swayed forwards down and then backwards up the terrace, served as a painful lesson in man-environment interaction.

Although the numbers attending football matches after the Second World War did not reach the peaks of the 1920s and 1930s, because of crowd-control policies, there was still a number of incidents in which people were killed because the pressure of numbers led to the collapse of various parts of the stadia. The most disastrous of these was when the support railings at Ibrox Stadium in Glasgow gave way when spectators who were leaving the ground fell on top of each other, leaving 68 dead. Other smaller incidents continued to occur, only to be overshadowed by the horrific disasters which took place in the space of a few weeks during the summer of 1985: the fire at Bradford City football ground, the collapse of a wall at Birmingham City, and the collapse of a wall in the Heysel Stadium in Brussels, with fatalities in each place.

The collapse of a wall at Heysel was the result of a near riot of rival spectators fighting each other. It served to highlight the association in the public mind between football and hooliganism. The series of near riots and general fracas that has occurred at football matches over the past ten years throughout the world has led to a link, in the media at least, between hooligans and football. Indeed a word-association test with many citizens would show that the word football was typically associated with the word hooligan.

We have looked as objectively as we can at the figures collected by many other people and at the reactions we have obtained from the ardent football supporters we have questioned. Furthermore, we started with the hypothesis commonly expressed in the social science literature that soccer violence is a minor problem, much exaggerated by the mass media. For example, the joint report of the Sports Council and Social Science Research Council came to the conclusion in 1978 that the scale of the problem was not large enough to warrant research attention.

As we have indicated, more recent researchers, notably sociologists at Leicester University, have pointed at groups in what they choose to call 'the rough working class' as the prime causes of football-related violence. We have no doubt about the validity of their claims. We also have no doubt that many football clubs are delighted with their findings because once again they help to exonerate the clubs and point a finger at some other agency – a good example of displacement theory in practice.

What has become clear to us in examining football violence in the context of emergencies within crowds is that all those so closely involved – the police, researchers and football authorities – have missed the most obvious point. The aggression we are talking about is centred around football matches. Of course, social and psychopathological processes play their part in these problems. However, football clubs can no more change the psychopathology of their supporters than they can change society. What they can change, however, is themselves.

A DESCENDING SPIRAL

We have already mentioned that we came to this conclusion from our data, having started with hypotheses that placed the problem in another context. The most telling part of these data was the combination of:

(a) steadily falling attendances
(b) steadily increasing arrest rates, within football grounds
(c) the relationship between arrest rates and casualties, and most importantly
(d) the frequency with which our respondents refer to the direct threat of violence as a reason for not going to matches more often.

It is important enough to repeat. We recognise that violence outside football grounds is a significant problem and that groups with criminal intent may well wish to use large crowds as a cover for their activities. Aggression and violence within stadia, though, are part of a distinct context. To use an ecological analogy, the context may be thought of as a habitat in which certain species are able to flourish because of the existence of certain conditions. These conditions are an interaction of individual, social, cultural and environmental factors. If the situation is to change then either these factors must be changed or their interrelationship.

The habitat metaphor alerts us to the poor condition of many football stadia, noticed and disliked by our respondents. Together with a large police presence and the perception of possible trouble the scene is set for a spiral of decay.

The perception of possible trouble contributes to this spiral probably more than actual incidents do. As we argued earlier, the withdrawal of support by those who abhor the possibility of violence leaves a setting more prone to aggression. When this perception is given validity by direct experience then the spiral is given another turn downwards.

Unfortunately, a process of target-hardening occurs in which groups become labelled and polarised. Police perceive a group of visiting supporters as 'troublemakers' and react accordingly. The group see this as a sign of aggression and respond in turn: the result is an escalation in perceived and actual aggression. Thus police strengthening which started out as an attempt to stop the spiral may only serve to lead to ever fiercer confrontations. Most commentators, whether from a social science or a law enforcement background, recognise that the segregation of fans has led to a clearer definition of opposing groups and has fed the distinctions out of which enmity so often grows. The barricades between parts of the ground, and separate ingress and egress routes, have provided further targets and challenges for violent action when it does erupt. Ironically, we have now reached such a position that any suggestion to remove these 'protections' is seen as a recipe for violence.

SOCIAL REPRESENTATION AS THE KEY

The need to control crowds and the fear of crowd violence, have led to a development in the already austere provision of football facilities that makes them look anything other than inviting places for leisure and recreation. Fences, gates, high walls, empty 'sterile' zones, have all been added to the provisions of football grounds, leading to a subtraction of their amenities. Seats have given way to concrete benches. Food containers, in which the meagre refreshments are sold, have to be lightweight plastic, virtually indistinguishable from much of the food that they contain. These places will soon only be attractive to the hardened enthusiast.

A continued reliance on these measures can only lead to their increase: stronger barriers, firmer segregation, the removal altogether of opposing fans and so on, would appear to be inevitable steps along a spiral of restraint. The only limiting factor will be the amount of constraint the majority of football supporters will tolerate before they stay home. Football clubs must now exert themselves if they are to attract a broader audience of interested spectators of all ages, of all backgrounds and both sexes.

It is argued by some that violence may be one reason why attendances at football matches have declined. It is probably a factor but little serious research has been undertaken to assess its effect. It is of obvious importance to distinguish between perceived and actual violence.

If violence is only one factor, what are the other contributory factors? It has been argued that more leisure time, increasing mobility and access to private transport, greater disposable income and family-orientated activities have led to a wider range of recreational pursuits. Some have also wondered why people should stand on a windy rain-swept terrace when they can watch the game on television in the comfort of their own homes? The Catch 22 corollary of this argument is the view that people have become satiated with football as a consequence of coverage on television. There is little doubt that these have been contributory factors. However, we would like to suggest two further reasons.

The first reason has received attention from writers such as Ingham[3] and is something which we have explored elsewhere in this book. Football used to be anchored very firmly in the local community from whence it secured its support. In many cases, players used to come from that community, as did the supporters. They identified with their local team. There was a sense in which the team represented their town or city and it was this identification and representation which contributed to the supporters' sense of place. The relationship between the supporters' social life, the activities they engaged in and where they engaged in them all contributed to the fans' self-identity. Within this framework there becomes a strong link between self and place.

In more recent years the communities around football clubs have changed substantially. The streets around Fulham Football Club, for example, used to be predominantly working-class. Over the last ten years this has changed as the area has been 'gentrified' and the houses become more up-market. Many of these new residents may see the existence of the club on their doorstep as a liability rather than an asset.

At the beginning of Alan Sillitoe's 'The Match'[4] the scene is set at Notts County football ground:

Towards the end of the match, when Bristol scored their winning goal, the players could only just be seen, and the ball was a roll of mist being kicked about the field. Advertising boards above the stands, telling of pork pies, ales, whisky, cigarettes and other delights of Saturday night, faded with the afternoon visibility.

Sillitoe, writing in 1954, captures well the setting and local world of football. This has now changed. At Notts County football ground today the advertising hoardings are now likely to pronounce the advantages of Italian truck companies, Japanese cameras or an American jean company. It is ironic that Notts County are sponsored by Wranglers, lying as they do at the centre of what was one of the major textile areas in Britain, and now suffering from substantial unemployment in the industry as a result of clothing imports from abroad.

This is not a misty-eyed, romantic and nostalgic longing for a world long since disappeared. It is simply an observation that the messages and meanings now being given in football grounds – by the grounds themselves – are very different to what they were thirty or even twenty years ago. The spectator is now being spoken to as a mass consumer, a member of a worldwide market for consumer goods. In some cases, the spectator may not even be an immediate consumer of those goods, where they refer to items such as lorries, as he was of 'pork pies and ale'. Indeed, the advertising hoardings are not addressing him but the unseen millions of television viewers at whom individual club sponsorship by commercial concerns is directed. Sponsorship is probably essential these days but one of the consequences is that the individuality and localness of clubs is disappearing.

Some might argue that sponsorship has only become essential because the pop-star ethos and culture which the entertainment industry has created and promoted amongst footballers has meant that clubs are forced into massive wage bills – for some players at least. Spectators see little evidence that the proceeds of sponsorship are channelled into ground improvements and the upgrading of spectator facilities. As with so much else about football, the spectator seems to be the last person to be considered. This may be a harsh and unfair criticism but to the man on the terrace who has to put up with unattractive, unpleasant and possibly not very safe conditions, such conclusions are almost unavoidable. If this is unreasonable, then more accountability as to how the proceeds of sponsorship deals are used by clubs would avoid this misperception.

One explanation we would give for the regular attendance at football matches by hundreds of thousands of loyal supporters, and for their attraction to the game, is that supporters identify with and have a pride in the team. The club's success is the supporters' success. Failure hurts. We would hypothesise that when there was a closer psychological and physical relationship between the football club and the surrounding community, the identification of the community with the club was strong. Supporters could bathe in the reflected glory of the club during times of success. In the world and culture in which football then existed, the activities of the local football club were one of the few opportunities for the working-class community to experience a sense of success and pride.

In the world in which we now live, *individual* success and ambition is held up as a normatively and universally desirable value. Walvin, perhaps quite rightly, criticises the notion that the prosperity of a few 'star' players has produced 'an unbridgeable gulf between footballers and their fans' and that this has led to alienation and, ultimately, hooliganism. Walvin[5] asserts that:

> The stars of today's professional game may well be out of reach
> of the rank and file fans, unlike the period up to the 1960s,
> but it has to be stressed that the great majority of professional
> footballers do not fall into this category; they remain within
> the social experience, geographical reach and sympathy of their
> supporters.

Objectively, this may well be the case. However, it might be argued that subjectively in the eyes of many football supporters this is not so. The popular image of footballers, one suspects, is that they lead fast, exciting 'pop-star' lives. Add to this another 'image' – that of a club management who are more concerned with money, sponsorship and 'big-name' players than the feelings of and facilities for their supporters. If this is the case and it has led to a lack of identification and a sense of alienation, it still remains to determine what the consequences of this are. One possible outcome for some supporters is violence. For others, it is just to stay away in their thousands. The club is no longer seen as representative of the community in the sense it was fifty years ago, and the consequent benefits of such identification are now absent for many. There are many alternative sources of satisfaction and success, which are orientated either towards the individual or the family. What sociologists refer to as the *embourgeoisement* of society is no less apparent in sport than other areas of our culture.

A second important reason, we believe, for a decline in football attendance is also tied up with place. Most football grounds are located in or near the centre of our cities, because that is where they have always been. There have been some attempts to move clubs out into greenfield sites where there is more space for other sports and social facilities but to date without much success. Watford Football Club have sought planning permission to move out of the town centre on a number of occasions and build a ground which would provide a range of sports and social facilities for the town but they have been continually thwarted by the local authority. So frustrated at the lack of progress were the club, they went to the expense (with financial assistance from the Football Trust) of building a railway halt – the first in the country in recent history – near the ground so that visiting supporters could be channelled away from the town centre.

Another recent case illustrates well all that is wrong with football. In 1982 Robert Maxwell, Chairman of Oxford United, announced that he had plans to buy Reading Football Club. The intention was to merge the two clubs, rename them the Thames Valley Royals and move the new club to a location between Oxford and Reading. Although Maxwell had discussed the matter with the Reading board of directors, the Reading board had not discussed it with the manager, players and least of all the paying and travelling supporters.[6] Some members of the board did oppose the merger and sought a High Court injunction to suspend share dealings between Maxwell and Frank Waller, the Chairman of Reading Football Club. Considerable opposition to the merger by the majority of shareholders, the supporters and some members of the board staved off the takeover, but not before Maxwell had made another attempt to take over Reading in the following season by offering shareholders five pounds for every fifty-pence share in an effort to secure a controlling interest in the club. Football clubs, like the products they advertise around the ground, are saleable commodities.

The Reading affair is not an isolated case. Charlton Athletic have recently had to leave The Valley because the owners of the ground acquired planning permission to build a supermarket on the site. The site became more valuable for the selling of groceries than for being the home of a once proud football club. Charlton Athletic now share a ground with Crystal Palace at Selhurst Park. Many former loyal Charlton Athletic supporters have refused to travel to the new ground and have ceased to support the club. Bristol Rovers play on the ground of Southern League team, Bath City, in the neighbouring town! For the spectator this leads to disenchantment and high travelling costs. Such moves might be more understandable and acceptable if they led to improvements in the facilities for supporters. It is doubtful whether this is the case, or whether this has even been a motivation.

The débâcle in early 1987 concerning the selling of Fulham's ground at Craven Cottage and the club's proposed amalgamation with Queens Park Rangers clearly demonstrated the strength of feeling amongst football supporters for a football team's home.

In this particular case, the club and its ground were being sold without any consultation with the supporters. The selling of the ground was not in response to a demand from supporters for improved facilities. It was simply a money-making exercise in which a football club just so happened to occupy valuable inner-city land. But there are cases where clubs want to move and so provide better access and better facilities for staff and supporters.

Clearly there is no easy solution, but whatever strategy is adopted it is important that change is driven by the needs and wishes of spectators, and that lessons from the Reading/Oxford and Fulham/QPR episodes are learnt.

Another aspect of place is the physical conditions to which supporters are subjected. Imagine the scene. The supporter has to park the car perhaps a mile from the football ground. As our supporter approaches the ground the police presence increases and the control over where and when he walks is increasingly limited. Given the size of the crowds such management is probably necessary and desirable. However, rather than being seen as an exercise in crowd control for the benefit of the crowd, the spectator has the feeling that he is seen as a potential miscreant and hooligan. The stance by police may be latently hostile and distancing rather than friendly and welcoming, inevitably leading to an atmosphere of deteriorating relations. Does it have to be like this at every match at every football ground?

Thus, the first experience for our supporter is one of control and hostility rather than a sense of welcome and value as a human being, let alone a consumer. Next, he pushes through a claustrophobic turnstile where he has the feeling of being processed like cattle rather than being a person with needs, wishes and sensitivities. He then stands on a wind and rain-swept bleak open terrace of cracked and crumbling steps for at least two hours. If lavatory facilities are provided, this usually means a breeze-block bunker, probably foul smelling and awash. Women are rarely catered for. The use of refreshment facilities will mean battling his way at half-time to a hut or hot-dog stand where tea is available. No culinary delights here.

The reader will have noticed that we have referred to the supporter as 'he'. We have pointedly made the same sexist assumption that football clubs make – that is, the football supporter is male. However, the proportion of females attending football matches is not insignificant. In a MORI poll conducted in 1985 in which a random sample of 2,069 people were asked how often they go to watch a football match at a League club, 4 per cent of females interviewed said they attended a match at least once a year, compared with 20 per cent of males. If this is an accurate reflection of the proportion of males and females who attend football matches, this would suggest that on average up to one-fifth of the people attending a Football League match are women. This is not greatly at variance with the 1983 *General Household Survey* which suggests that 1 person in 6 attending a Football League match is female.

In what other recreational activity would people tolerate such conditions? The surprising thing is that people are actually prepared to pay to be subjected to such an experience, although fewer and fewer supporters are now doing so. How much longer will football supporters tolerate this treatment before they stay at home or choose to watch other sports?

REVERSING THE SPIRAL

To reverse the spiral something radical is necessary and a number of clubs are beginning to examine the possibilities. Two major objectives must be both to change the image of football and to change the way football is currently experienced by the public. In the current social science jargon, it is the social representation that needs to be changed. Clearly, improving football ground facilities is an important part of this exercise. Such improvements can only come about when something far more important and deep-rooted is changed – attitudes: the attitudes of football supporters as to what they are prepared to tolerate in terms of the spectating conditions at our national game; the attitudes of club management to their responsibilities and the facilities which they should provide for their customers; the attitudes of all those involved in the club and those in the community in which the football stadium is located; and the attitudes of the media, whose policy is often one of putting the bad news about football on the front page of newspapers and the good news on the back page.

This change can be achieved by means of both 'hard' and 'soft' management. 'Hard' management focuses on improvements to the physical fabric of football grounds, and the crowd control strategies which are used by the police and ground officials. 'Soft' management attempts to change attitudes by means of an educational process. Hard and soft management techniques necessarily interact with each other. Attitude change is not going to come about overnight. Some of the proposals we put forward will need to be implemented over a number of years, while others should and could be addressed more immediately. Later in this chapter we specify the sort of action that needs to be undertaken by Football League clubs, the football authorities, the Home Office, the Department of the Environment and the police in both the short and long term. These proposals take the form of a checklist.

In the remainder of this final chapter, we discuss six major areas of activity which comprise a positive strategy for dealing with the current crisis in British football.

The first is trying to change the nature of a football match as it is experienced by spectators. The second focuses on providing a safe environment for spectators of all ages and physical abilities. The third is the linking of the management of the club much more closely to its supporters. The fourth is building stronger connections between all those involved in the club and those in the community in which the football stadium is located. The fifth, drawing on the previous issues, is to encourage the media to proclaim the success and enjoyments of being a spectator as loudly as they proclaim the discomforts. The sixth is making the public in general and the football supporter in particular more aware of their football heritage.

We provided a scenario of what it is currently like to attend a football match. We would now like to describe an alternative scenario – a strategy which has as its central tenet the notion of 'caring for the spectator', whereby resources and effort are channelled into providing the football-going spectator with a satisfactory series of experiences. Whether we are talking about a trip to a theatre, the circus or a tourist attraction, the consumer is looking for a pleasurable outing in attractive and comfortable surroundings. They are looking to be entertained, to spend money on food, drink and souvenirs of what should be a memorable experience. There is no reason why football cannot adopt the same criteria and aspirations. Furthermore, returning to our earlier propositions, a sense of identity and a sense of place must again become essential components of the world of football.

THE FOOTBALL EXPERIENCE AND CARING FOR THE SPECTATOR

Clubs must be geared up to provide not only what the directors, shareholders, management and players want, and what they believe the spectator wants, but what the spectator actually wants. Football management must put itself in the shoes of the spectator and *care for them*. Football management must strive to make it easy for the spectator to get the most out of their visit to a football match from the time they make a decision to attend, to the moment they arrive at the turnstile. This 'caring for the spectator' does not come easy – it must be a clearly thought-out strategy. At the centre of this caring approach is a recognition that the spectator is a valued customer or client, who should be treated with respect and consideration.

The first essential step is to know the spectator – who he *and* she is, where he or she comes from, what he or she wants. It is not enough for management to assume they know. Constant appraisal, for example, by means of surveys is essential. The image of the football supporter as the middle-aged male in a flat cap (when it is not a teenager with Doc Martin boots) is totally at variance with all the research evidence. The 1983 General Household Survey examined the socioeconomic characteristics of spectators at football matches four weeks prior to the survey. The largest proportion of spectators was either in the professional, employers or managerial group (4 per cent) or the skilled manual group (4 per cent). Intermediate and junior non-manual (2 per cent) and semi-skilled and unskilled made up the smaller proportions. In terms of age, 8 per cent of 16–34 year olds attended a football match within the four weeks prior to the interview compared with 6 per cent of 35–59 year olds and 2 per cent of those over 60 years of age.

Football management must look after their paying spectators as does any other high-quality visitor attraction. If the football stadium and the football experience were to be construed as part of the repertory of leisure and recreation attractions available to the public, very different standards of provision and service would be expected and provided. If going to a football match were to be seen like attending the theatre or visiting a tourist attraction, certain assumptions would be made about what the consumer requires from the visit, what satisfactions need to be provided for and what would be the consequences of the failure to meet these assumptions. It is part of the everyday assessment of highly professional facilities in the tourism and leisure business to ask questions such as what sort of visitors are we trying to attract? What sort of experience should we be providing for visitors? What are their needs, wishes, satisfactions? How do we attract the first-time visitor? How do we encourage repeat visitation? Spectator can be substituted for visitor in each case without any difficulty. If clubs are not prepared to answer these questions then they might as well play behind closed gates as West Ham United had to do several seasons ago as a consequence of crowd trouble.

If clubs start to respond to questions such as these (and their response is backed up with investment), the quality of football grounds and the quality of the football experience for the spectator will undergo a radical transformation. Some clubs have started along this road but there is still a long way to go. It is as if football management are partially aware of what needs to be done but are hidebound by tradition, inertia, financial constraints and a lack of appropriate skills and expertise. What will this mean in practice? One option might be for clubs to sell off their valuable, congested and often decrepit inner-city grounds and move either to the outskirts of our urban areas where more land is available for the development of sporting, social and community facilities, or to low-value, inner-city derelict land sites which need reclamation. Even within some of our larger cities and conurbations there are hundreds of acres of derelict land which are looking for a positive use.

The visitor should arrive relaxed and looking forward to an enjoyable afternoon's entertainment. Everything should be done to make the spectator's journey as easy as possible. On arrival at key arrival points – car parks, railway stations and bus stations – there should be orientation panels which inform visiting spectators where the ground is and where they can buy food and drink. Given the availability of land, car parks should be provided wherever possible and must be clean, well surfaced and landscaped in an attractive way. This would then be supported by a comprehensive signing system, perhaps in the club colours, to take spectators directly to the ground while at the same time minimising disruption to the rest of the community. Having arrived at the ground, there must be a sense of welcome so that the spectator is made to feel a valued consumer and a valued human being. The entrance sign is important and must clearly advertise what the football club offers its spectators and why an afternoon at a football match is an exciting event.

The environment is continually providing us with messages and meanings: it says something about how those who own or manage places see those who use them. If the environment is unattractive and unwelcoming, it will stimulate negative if not hostile responses. A well-designed and managed environment which encourages a positive response and attitude should not be seen as an optional luxury but as an essential requirement of all sports and leisure facilities. Perhaps the most important change of all that can be brought about involves increasing the amount of face-to-face contact with the club and ground staff. A personal welcome is important, and it is remembered. This is most effectively done at the entrance point into the ground or at the turnstile. It may seem absurd that one could even contemplate welcoming 20,000 spectators individually to a football ground. However, clubs like Watford do try to welcome everybody who comes through the turnstile. When the spectator gets into the ground they are given a programme or Cup match vouchers by a smiling steward: children entering the Sir Stanley Rous Stand are given a packet of crisps. While this is only a small and inexpensive gesture, its public relations value is considerable.

Staff training is fundamental and often underrated. Investment in 'facing the public' can repay itself many times over if it achieves the right response from the spectator. It will also involve a change in the relationship of the club staff and stewards to those who attend matches or travel to other grounds to support their team. Stewards should be trained in all aspects of people management, not just people movement. They should be able to deal not only with issues such as crowd control, safety and first aid, but also all those aspects of public relations which we call 'caring for the spectator'.

The provision of food and drink is important. It should not just be a token gesture but a quality service. It should cater for all markets from tea and sandwiches at half-time to more substantial facilities such as restaurants. Chelsea is one club which is trying to offer snack facilities on a more professional basis than is typically found at many grounds. Some clubs such as Coventry City make maximum use of their investment in catering by offering 'out of hours' evening catering as well. The planning and economics of catering are as specialised as football management. Suffice it to say that 'value for money' catering with good quality food, friendly staff and attractive sales outlets in pleasant surroundings is essential.

It is ironic that in the current political climate, it is the private sector which is constantly held up as the pacesetter for the provision of entrepreneurial facilities such as catering. Yet one has to turn to the public sector for examples of innovation in this area. For example, the provision of restaurant and snack facilities at the South Bank improved out of all recognition in recent years under the management of the 'late' Greater London Council. British Rail's catering operation which used to be the stuff of music-hall jokes has been transformed by their seeking the advice and expertise of Prue Leith. British Rail now even offer regional menus on some of their trains. There is no reason why football clubs cannot do the same.

Clubs do not have to run catering facilities themselves. With a captive audience of 20,000 or even 5,000 a match, there ought to be a number of opportunities for offering catering as a concession. This could be either to a local company or perhaps to a national catering chain who could negotiate with the Football League a contract to provide refreshments and catering at a number of grounds. It would be in the interest of the concessionaire to offer a good service, and clubs could insist on quality control. By giving clubs a percentage of the profit, it would benefit clubs to promote the facility (and thereby themselves) and make it a success.

Clubs are now developing their souvenir shops. For example, the shop adjacent to Manchester United's stadium carries an extensive stock. There is, however, still scope for expansion. Leisure shopping is a major income generator. In many tourist attractions, shop sales can account for 20 per cent or more of the income. In 1981, shop sales in historic houses accounted for approximately 23 per cent of the total income, while a further 20 per cent was derived from catering. Across tourism attractions as a whole, research on visitor expenditure on day trips suggested that in 1982 over 60 per cent of visitor expenditure on a day trip was spent on food and drink, while this increased to 75 per cent when gifts and souvenirs are taken into account. Ever since Walt Disney built Disneyland around a parade of shops, the tourism and leisure industry has recognised that ancillary sales are not only an important source of income but also an essential part of the day out for visitors.

Football clubs have a lot to learn. One could imagine the club shop selling not only souvenirs such as the club strip, towels and knick-knacks related to the particular club, but leisure wear, sports equipment, books on football, and it could even operate as a travel agency. There are considerations such as the cost of initial stocking but arrangements can be made with local sports shops, bookshops and others to provide goods on a sale or return basis. Equally, the shop could be run as a concession. These arrangements are entered into every day by other sectors of the tourism and leisure industry. The one distinct advantage that football clubs have, which many leisure facilities do not, is the great amount of space in and around the grounds. But they also have another distinct advantage – the club culture we discussed in Chapter 3. They could be literally cashing in on the uniqueness of their own particular club in terms of the shops it has and the merchandise it sells.

We believe that there are many opportunities for clubs to improve the standard of comfort and the range of services for spectators and the community. As with issues discussed later concerning health and safety, various bodies can respond to this need. Of course, conditions of comfort necessarily interact with health and safety, and should be seen in such a context.

The football authorities should bring together all those who are responsible for promoting, playing and managing the sport (including the Football Associations, the Football Leagues, the Professional Footballers' Association and others) in order to provide resources and practical advice on how to achieve the objectives we have outlined in order to improve the experience of going to a football match. We would envisage that the football authorities will need to draw on skills and advice from individuals and organisations not currently involved in sport in general or football in particular.

The general ambience of football grounds needs to be upgraded through internal improvements and by good maintenance. This includes the provision of better surfacing of terraces, steps and the general fabric of football grounds, clean lavatories and wet weather protection at a minimum. This involves an attitude of mind as much as a financial commitment on the part of football management. All the facilities and services which are provided for the benefit of spectators should receive the same careful planning and attention to detail as pre-match preparation for the players. They all make up the total football experience.

The football authorities should not only recognise poor provision of facilities and punish disruptive behaviour by members of the public but should also reward positive initiatives on the part of clubs and their supporters. This has happened through the Canon sponsorship of the Football League, but other methods and rewards could also be explored.

SAFETY AND CROWD CONTROL

We have been at pains to point out that our interest in this matter is not just a concern for the future of our national sport. Safety and crowd control were at the centre of our study's terms of reference for the Popplewell Inquiry. At present it appears that responsibility for all aspects of safety and related matters of crowd control at football clubs is split between a number of different people. One person within the club may have the job of going around with the fire officer to check escape routes. Another person may be responsible for matters of maintenance relating to barriers and other aspects of the physical conditions. In practice, if not in theory, the police are likely to have overall responsibility for crowd egress and segregation.

The responsibility of stewards and others who serve the spectators (such as food franchises) whose activities may carry safety implications may be quite distinct from other responsibilities in relation to safety. Indeed, in many cases stewards appear to see their role as guiding people to their places or opening or closing exit routes. They are likely to be informed of the location of fire extinguishers and have general instruction on their actions with regard to opening doors in an emergency. Their responsibility for taking an active role in the prevention of dangerous incidents or reporting on possible problems is often not so clear.

As far as can be ascertained, few clubs have appointed a specifically designated safety officer or manager who is a senior member of the club, either a director or specifically responsible to a director. Such a person would have the authority, recognised within the club, to liaise with all the people concerned noted above. They could become a partisan voice within the club for safety matters. While at present all senior individuals within a club will support the virtues of safety, they will be constrained by the other demands on resources, of which they are aware, when arguing for improved safety. An individual who has the concern for safety as his prime responsibility is therefore likely to take a different approach to the problem.

A safety manager could also embrace the consideration of comfort. Comfort and safety interconnect in many important ways. An example of this is the provision of ramps instead of steps. Although ramps are often provided with wheelchair and disabled users in mind, they are often preferred by able-bodied people. It would be appropriate to build ramps rather than steps in some parts of football grounds. Not only would these be preferred by the public but they would also be safer, as there would be less chance of people tripping up when moving up or down in a large crowd. The demonstration by clubs of their direct concern for spectators would go some way to alleviate the criticisms often directed at them. It may even reduce minor acts of vandalism or aggression that are the product of dissatisfaction with the club.

There are a number of detailed recommendations in respect of health and safety issues which we submitted as part of our evidence to the *Committee of Inquiry into Crowd Safety and Control at Sports Grounds* for Mr Justice Popplewell. Some of them have been enshrined in government guidelines or statute but it is worth emphasising that these actions can be undertaken by the football clubs themselves, the football authorities, the Home Office, Department of the Environment and the police.

In the short term, Football League clubs should establish training programmes. These should comprise training films, talks, demonstrations, role-playing exercises involving the police, medical services, the fire brigade and stewards. We also suggest that a training guide is written which covers issues such as safety, comfort, emergency action, staff training and the appointment of a safety manager.

With the sophisticated technology which is now available, crowd management should be easier. For example, segmented public address systems could be installed throughout grounds, which allows some or all loudspeakers to be operated at any one time thus enabling the controlled management of crowd movement. This could be supported by the installation of closed-circuit television, permitting a centralised overview and management of crowd movement. Chelsea Football Club has been at the forefront of this type of initiative.

The football authorities need to provide guidance to football clubs on all aspects of safety and comfort in football stadia, so that there are minimum standards and a nationally agreed procedure for dealing with emergency and evacuation procedures. These procedures should be public and available to supporters, so that they have prior knowledge of them. The football authorities should also sponsor and organise training programmes covering comfort and safety in football stadia as outlined above, i.e. training films, talks, demonstrations, and the production of a training guide covering safety, comfort and emergency action. The improvement of football grounds – their physical fabric and standards of safety and comfort – will require a massive injection of capital and revenue funding. The football authorities should provide advice to clubs, or seek the assistance of others, on how to raise capital and create an environment in which private investment and sponsorship, trust funding and, where appropriate, public-sector funding become available to projects. The Football Trust has an essential role to play here.

Centralised records should be established of all football matches, listing crowd sizes and police deployment as well as incidents relating to football matches. These should include details of arrests, convictions, ejections and casualties. They should also include details of all fires and malicious damage. This was one of the major recommendations of the 1978 joint SSRC/Sports Council report; the need for this is still present. Any incidents should be followed by an inquiry, the report of which is made public.

If training manuals and films on crowd control are not already available they should be produced. Such training material should take account of the growing social psychological material on crowd behaviour under normal and emergency conditions. Liaison with football clubs should be extended to cover regular briefings of stewards and other staff on duty at matches. Wherever possible the police should encourage stewards and other ground staff to take the primary responsibility for as many aspects of crowd control as possible.

The Home Office and the Department of the Environment also have an important role to play. For example, they should commission research on crowd movement and densities at football and other sports grounds and stadia. This should relate the physical parameters and conditions to the experiences of the crowds. Research needs to be undertaken on how crowds respond to different forms of instruction and warning under different circumstances. We know comparatively little about the development and context of actual violent events. Such research could be modelled on the productive work that has been conducted into behaviour in emergencies.[7] This should include a consideration of the different ethos or culture of each club.

It is unreasonable to expect that the many people involved in a football ground will be able to perform all that might be demanded of them in an emergency without (a) having been informed in detail what could be required, and (b) having some opportunity to try out the appropriate actions as part of an overall drill or practice. The training of all staff is therefore essential. One might also add that training in itself has all sorts of social and psychological value. It can create a sense of belonging and involvement, strengthen group loyalty and identity, instil camaraderie and generally improve interpersonal relations within the organisation. Most importantly, the carrying out of training exercises can show that management is committed to safe practices and cares about spectators.

THE FOOTBALL CLUB AND ITS SUPPORTERS

The third component involves full participation by supporters in the club's activities. There are advantages and disadvantages to instituting a membership scheme. One of the key benefits is that it would strengthen members' identification and even responsibility for the club's affairs as well as providing rights to attend matches.

The term 'club' would then come closer to its dictionary definition of an association of people with common aims and interests. Tottenham Hotspur have taken this one stage further and made the club a publicly quoted, limited company on the Stock Exchange, thereby allowing supporters to readily buy and sell shares in the club. In this way, the directors are much more accountable to their supporters if those supporters are also shareholders. This does, at least theoretically, give supporters some control over the future development of the club. Only time will tell if this is anything more than tokenism. It is, however, an interesting experiment which is worth monitoring.

Traditionally, supporters' clubs have attempted to fulfil this role. The benefits of joining a supporters' club, though, have often been more psychological than practical. It has enabled supporters to feel a closer identity with their club. A supporters' club member is an 'official' supporter and may therefore feel somehow rather better than the person who just pays at the gate and is an otherwise anonymous member of the crowd. To be fair many supporters' clubs have bars where supporters can have a drink before or after the match, or during the week when there are no matches. They have also offered discounted travel to away matches.

In recent years, though, supporters' clubs have also been seen as a device for screening supporters. Sanctions are, however, limited. It is likely that different groups of supporters will perceive the supporters' club differently. For some, it is a social club and an additional means of expressing support. For others, especially those who cause trouble at grounds, joining a supporters' club would probably be the last thing they would contemplate, seeing it as representing the status quo and an instrument of authority.

The membership scheme being adopted by some clubs could be seen as an extension of the supporters' club idea, although the way it has been presented by football clubs demonstrates that it is more to do with control and containment rather than identity and support. Even after all the criticism that has been levelled at the management of football, it is remarkable that even this exercise has been poorly handled with an eye to public relations and image. To be fair to football clubs, though, membership schemes have been imposed on clubs by the government with little regard to the consequences or effectiveness of such actions. There is much to recommend a membership scheme but people will only become members of a club if they have a strong sense of identity with it and a feeling that it is worth while joining. In terms of what is on offer at many football grounds today this is surely questionable.

The kind of improved conditions described in this chapter would make it easier to attract a membership. Active pursuit of a participating membership naturally establishes links with the community. This in turn presents opportunities for clubs to offer a range of facilities that might be attractive to such a membership and thereby maximise the return on the financial investment. This could include the provision of all-weather playing and training surfaces, restaurants, entertaining and meeting-room facilities, or even discos under the stands, which is happening at Oldham Athletic. An involved membership provides a human and financial resource in the context of which the ground conditions and associated facilities can develop, and thereby attract more members.

THE FOOTBALL CLUB AND THE COMMUNITY

Many different links between clubs and their local community have been encouraged by the Sports Council and other bodies and there is little doubt that some clubs are trying to forge such closer ties with the community. A thorough investigation of the successes and failures of the schemes supported by the Sports Council has been conducted by Ingham of Southampton University[8]. His report does indicate that these schemes have achieved some degree of success but that improvements in monitoring them could result in even more benefits.

A few years ago the Wildfowl Trust at Slimbridge attracted national publicity when it promoted an 'Adopt a duck' scheme. Visitors could adopt a duck for a small sum of money, and the Trust would keep them informed about 'their' duck even to the extent of receiving postcards from it! The principle behind this scheme has been taken up in many other places by a range of organisations as a means of fund-raising. Football clubs, too, have seen the potential: it is now possible to sponsor footballers, or rather their kit. At Watford Football Club, it currently costs £150 to sponsor the complete kit, £40 for a pair of match boots, £40 for a match kit and so on. There is no shortage of sponsors. Such an activity not only encourages involvement and interest but is also good for fund-raising and public relations.

For younger supporters, Watford have initiated a 'Junior Hornets

Sportsworld' scheme. In this, first team players hold coaching sessions on various aspects of the game such as goalkeeping and outfield play. The scheme has been so successful that Watford are extending the scheme to include other sports besides football.

If football grounds are to be recognised as a community resource, and more importantly, football clubs are seen as an important part of the social and cultural life of the community, then there is a strong case for encouraging more direct contact between schools and clubs. There are opportunities for the intelligent study of football as a social, cultural, economic and sporting activity. Furthermore, current educational initiatives do exist which football clubs could respond to and benefit from in terms of public relations and community involvement in the short term, and attitude changes and the enlistment of public support in the longer term. Football clubs could appoint an Education Officer and provide classroom/meeting-room facilities, along with pupil and teacher resource material and other resources. Such an innovatory formal and informal educational programme could also generate income. It may be possible for the local education authority to second a teacher to the football club, in which case the cost to the club would be minimal.

Some clubs might not see education as their business: why should they bear this unnecessary and unacceptable cost? If clubs do not look seriously at proposals such as these, then the costs of disaffection and loss of the next generation of spectators could be much greater. There are a number of educational programmes which have been launched in recent years which are relevant to the type of initiative being proposed here. A brief summary of these initiatives will demonstrate the opportunities for this potential gearing between football, education and training and the ways in which football can have vocational and skill relevance.

The Technical, Vocational and Education Initiative (TVEI) is a four-year project for 14–18 year olds which is run on a modular basis as an alternative to GCE and CSE examinations. The objective is to give increased practical technical and vocational training. With its emphasis on technology and business studies, this has obvious application to the modern world of professional football. The courses are based on City and Guilds of London Institute 365, which has a compulsory social, economic and environment module, and Business and Technical Education Council (BTEC) Examinations.

The Certificate in Pre-Vocational Education (CPVE) is another initiative, launched in September 1985. It is a one-year course, embracing a transition from generalised to vocational education and employment. Work in core areas such as communications, science, knowledge about industrial society and personal and creative development are complemented by vocational and structured work experience. The CPVE is administered by a Joint Board of the two principal validating bodies for pre-vocational education, the City and Guilds of London Institute and the Business and Technical Education Council (BTEC), and offers modules related to specific 'occupational families' of which the environment and urban studies, etc., is one. There is a specific module on tourism, recreation and environmental issues. The study of all aspects of football would be a worthwhile unit within such a module, providing students with a practical and meaningful case study.

The General Certificate of Secondary Education (GCSE) is perhaps the most significant development in education in recent years bringing together GCE and CSE and aims to capture the 40 per cent of pupils who are not at present caught in that combined net. It started in September 1986 and will incorporate a 'project' comprising 20 per cent of the marks for most of the major subjects (biology, geography, history, craft design and technology). An example might be environmental or social science work on some aspect of recreation planning or issue-based work very similar to that already undertaken at A level in the 16–19 geography project. Pupils are encouraged by teachers to tackle something local and it is not difficult to conceive of classes of pupils examining the catchment area from which a football club draws support, the socioeconomic characteristics of the football-going public, the economics of running a football club, or the logistics of managing a large crowd in order to ensure safety and comfort. Pupils could approach the local planning department, libraries, archivists, the police, and St John's Ambulance Brigade, in order to collect information and come to a closer understanding of football, its management and organisation.

The most recent initiative which has relevance to developing the educational role of football clubs in the community is that of the proposed City Technology Colleges announced by the Rt Hon. Kenneth Baker, Secretary of State for Education in October 1986. These will offer a broad curriculum with a strong technical and practical element. They will be set up exclusively in urban areas, especially inner cities and those areas experiencing social deprivation where there is already on-going government support such as through the Inner City Initiative. It is noteworthy that of the twenty or more possible locations already identified for City Technology Colleges, all have at least one long-established local football team, and some have several.

It is quite clear from the above that the environment and the world of work and leisure in its broadest sense is receiving more attention in the school curriculum. In particular, these initiatives offer the opportunity to study the local area and local issues. There is no reason why all aspects of professional football – as a sport, business, recreational and leisure activity, and its associated technology – could not respond to these curricular developments.

Football should be seen as part of the leisure and recreation industry and of education in the way we have advocated. There is every precedent for these types of initiatives. There are many tourist and visitor attractions throughout the country which have extensive Training Agency schemes providing job opportunities in areas of high unemployment. On- and off-the-job training can be an integral part of many of these schemes. Football provides an opportunity to bring together education, training and community involvement with leisure and recreational activities.

FOOTBALL AND THE MEDIA

Football is shy about its achievements. More football clubs need to appoint press and public relations officers, if only on a part-time/voluntary basis, to make the media more aware of the good things about football and their contribution to the social, cultural, sporting and economic life of the community. Such an appointment would force clubs to think about what they are doing and turn such activities into positive news stories. If clubs are not doing anything newsworthy, it would encourage them to think about what they should be doing.

Football's image has been tarnished for too long because its spokesmen could only speak in clichés, expressing their current psychological state as being either 'as sick as a parrot' or 'over the moon'. Football must present itself through the media in such a way that its spokesmen (hopefully some spokeswomen) are articulate and provide an insight into the game with an intelligent commentary. Trevor Brooking, Jimmy Hill, Ian St John and Jimmy Greaves have done much to redress the balance.

Football needs more imaginative marketing. Cricket has responded to a decline in interest and increasing competition from other leisure and recreation pursuits by introducing first-class, one-day cricket matches which fit fairly comfortably within television schedules. These not only receive massive television audiences but they also fill the grounds full of spectators. Football has tried five-a-side football and various minor cup matches but without much success. There must be other types of matches which could capture the football-going and more importantly the non-football-going public's imagination. Some of the top football clubs have been discussing for some time the notion of a Super League. Perhaps a Super League at the end of the season featuring the top clubs in England, Scotland, Wales and Northern Ireland to determine the British champions would meet the interests of clubs and the public. The interest generated by the League play-offs at the end of the 1986–7 season supports this notion. An international 'Festival of Football' in which the top League clubs from Europe compete in a European League would not only add sparkle to the league programme but might go some way to persuade FIFA to allow English clubs to play in European competitions again.

To many people, football is selfish and inward looking. At a time of declining gates, flagging public interest and a poor media image, introversion and retrenchment is not the solution. Football needs to put across a strong message demonstrating that it has much to offer the community and society.

The media is increasingly influenced by photographic images and what is visual and presentable in a simple direct way. It is essential that the football clubs and the footballing institutions provide them with new images that replace those that dominate at present. Many of the proposals that we are putting forward are newsworthy in themselves.

THE FOOTBALL HERITAGE

The present-day football supporter has inherited a footballing heritage that goes back more than 100 years. Indeed, the 1987–8 season was the centenary of the formation of the Football League. Such an event was a marvellous opportunity for the Football League to launch a major series of publicity and educational events telling the story of football's heritage. The story of football from its earliest days to its growth into the world's most popular sport deserves to be told: the history of the FA Cup; the development of the first British clubs like the Wanderers (Wolverhampton Wanderers), Small Heath (Birmingham City) and Royal Arsenal (Arsenal); the disappearance of clubs such as Accrington Stanley, Workington Town, and Southport. The decline in the industrial heartlands has seen a new pattern of successful clubs not based in the industrial cities of the North and West Midlands but in the Home Counties (Watford, Wimbledon, Luton), East Anglia (Ipswich, Norwich) and the south coast (Southampton, Portsmouth and Brighton). The changing geography of football; the history of individual clubs; the story of famous managers, players, referees, grounds, matches, incidences, are all worth recounting. This all makes up the heritage of football.

At this point, it is perhaps worth while rehearsing some of the arguments which have been put forward for informing the public about our rich national and cultural heritage. The conservation movement has learnt that, if people are to appreciate and conserve the heritage, they must be informed about it in interesting and entertaining ways. It is argued that a widespread understanding and appreciation of the importance of heritage is the most sound insurance against insensitive and antipathetic developments. If mass public support for conservation is not enlisted then we will lose our heritage. The discussion about football in the context of heritage conservation is not totally misplaced: the case for public education applies no less to football than it does to our castles and national parks. Football has suffered enormously over the past few years from a variety of ills. What it needs now is mass public support for its resuscitation and development – otherwise attending football matches will be simply a memory.

Football has a rich heritage which represents an asset not a liability. It is an asset which could be built upon to enhance the experience of spectators who attend football matches and to tackle some of the problems which are facing football in the light of an increasingly exasperated and intolerant society.

The professional activity which seeks to tell the story of our heritage to the public with a view to informing them and changing their attitudes and behaviours is called interpretation[9]. The objectives of interpretation are to increase understanding, enhance enjoyment, and engender a sense of caring and respect for the environment. In conservation terms, interpretation is seen as having a key role to play in minimising damage caused by public access to fragile environments and ecologically sensitive areas. Freeman Tilden[10] (1957) defined interpretation as 'an educational activity which aims to reveal meanings and relationships through the use of original objects, by first-hand experience, and by illustrative media, rather than to simply communicate factual information'. This can be achieved by means of exhibitions, trails, audio-visual shows, theatre, interpretive panels, events, leaflets and booklets at heritage sites.

There is no reason why individual football clubs could not tell their story to their supporters by these means. Informative panels about the history of the club and its successes, its players and officials could be located around the ground. Leaflets and guides to the club and its organisation could be produced. A video or tape-slide programme about the club could be taken around to community groups, interest groups and schools, thereby strengthening community ties. A 'guided walk' or trail around the ground could be available on non-match days. Theatres, such as the Barbican and the National Theatre, offer this service because they have recognised that they have a resource which is under-utilised for large parts of the day. Furthermore, large numbers of people are interested in seeing 'backstage'. In response, these theatres offer guided tours of all parts of the theatre, including 'backstage', props room, and stars' dressing-rooms. This not only makes the theatre-going experience more interesting for the public but it also is good public relations and generates income. Guided tours are available at Cardiff Arms Park (rugby) and Wembley, so there is clearly a demand within sport for such a development.

Manchester United have recognised the opportunities in this area by opening a small museum, with a range of interesting displays about the history of the club and its achievements in domestic and international competitions. These displays comprise various football memorabilia, including trophies and cups, England caps, football jerseys, and programmes of famous matches. This material is supported by exhibition panels of text and photographs which tell the story of the club, with videos of famous players and matches. The

Munich air crash was such a traumatic event in the club's history that there is a major display about the disaster: it is almost a shrine. It includes photographs and copies of the newspapers of the day which reported the tragedy. The Manchester United museum will attract anyone interested in football, and attempts to interest those who know little about the subject. A substantial number of school parties visits the exhibition, demonstrating the educational potential of the museum and the opportunity to achieve the type of attitude and behaviour change advocated elsewhere in this chapter.

This is not an isolated example of a sport recognising that people do have a thirst for information and stimulation, and that with imagination, effort and investment it is possible to unlock the heritage of our world-famous national pastime. Other sports which have sought to tell their stories by means of museums and exhibitions are rugby (Cardiff Arms Park) horse racing (Newmarket) and tennis (Wimbledon).

There is any number of opportunities for clubs to engage in these sorts of activities which would create positive links between the management of the club and the supporters, and the club and the surrounding community. The history and heritage of football is an extremely valuable asset which can be used to restore pride, create a sense of identity and belonging, enlist public support and enhance the spectator's appreciation and enjoyment of the sport.

CHANGING GROUNDS AND CHANGING ATTITUDES

Football is now facing competition from the entertainment and leisure industry to a degree it has never before experienced. Football will eventually have to come to terms with this competition through a change in attitude and the promotion of an image which sees football and its facilities as a recreational resource for the community, which has to be managed and marketed like any other income-earning, private-sector visitor attraction. The *concept* of football as an exciting spectator sport for all ages should be backed up by *products* which reinforce the concept and image. We have discussed above some of the types of product that are possible.

Starting with the physical conditions of a ground has many advantages. Football grounds carry symbolic as well as functional implications. Unfortunately, tackling the physical conditions in grounds has typically meant stronger barriers, firmer segregation and the creation of what is called 'sterile areas'. At Luton this has been taken to such an extreme that supporters of opposing teams are now banned from the ground. Such a policy tied up with a membership scheme has been actively promoted by the government. Whatever the motivations of individuals for introducing such a scheme, one has to question whether such a decision is in the long-term interest of football clubs or their supporters, given what we know about the football-going habits of the public reported earlier.

A continued reliance on measures such as these can only lead to their increase, and an escalation in 'hard' management methods of restraint. The only limiting factor will be the amount of constraint the majority of football supporters will tolerate before they stay at home. Keeping the rain off the spectators, providing them with seats and reasonable food are clearly acts of a club that cares about its supporters. Furthermore, such modifications are highly visible and there for all to see and photograph, publish and discuss. Although much of this book has concentrated on changing and improving the physical conditions at football grounds, we argue most strongly that such improvements must be seen in the context of football clubs changing their image and changing their perceptions and attitudes towards the supporter. Likewise the public needs to become more critical and demanding of the type of experience football currently provides.

There will obviously be an important interaction between changing the physical facilities and changing attitudes. The measures adopted so far by football clubs have either been piecemeal, ineffective or half-hearted and, we believe, fail to address the real issues in any meaningful way. The 'solutions' which are currently being forced upon football smack of panic measures which will ultimately do more harm than good to football. What is being advocated here does not necessarily require a major injection of finance, although there will be a need to compensate for the under-investment and capitalisation that football has experienced over the last forty years. More importantly, we are talking about the use of skills, resources and experience which are readily available in the local community, in the recreation industry and in education, to reverse what at present seems like a terminal illness. To repeat again the words of Bill Shankley, 'Some people think football is as important as life and death. I can assure them that it is much more serious than that.'

NOTES

INTRODUCTION: BACKGROUND AND BEGINNINGS
1 *Public Disorder and Sporting Events*, Sports Council/Social Science Research Council, 1978.
2 *Committee of Inquiry into Crowd Safety and Control at Sports Grounds. Final Report*, Chairman: Mr Justice Popplewell, HMSO: London, 1986, Cmnd 9710.

CHAPTER 1 FOUR THEMES
1 Population Censuses and Surveys Office, *The General Household Survey*, HMSO: London, 1983.
2 Canter, D. and Wools, R., 'A Technique for the Subjective Evaluation of Buildings', *Building Science*, vol. 5, pp. 113–18, 1974.
3 Trivizas, E., 'Sentencing the Football Hooligan', *British Journal of Criminology*, 21(4), pp. 342–9, 1981.
4 Ibid.

CHAPTER 2 SPECTATORS' VIEWS
1 Further technical details are presented in D. Canter, et al., 'Psychological Aspects of Crowd Safety and Control at Football Grounds. A Report Presented to the Committee of Inquiry into Crowd Safety and Control at Sports Grounds. Chairman: Mr Justice Popplewell', University of Surrey: Guildford, September 1985.

CHAPTER 3 CLUB CULTURES
1 Inglis, B., *The Football Grounds of England and Wales*, Willow Books: London, 1985.
2 Canter, D., *Facet Theory*, Springer: New York, 1985.
3 Duffield, B., 'Crowd Behaviour: The Scottish Experience', in *Football as a Focus for Disorder*, Centre for Contemporary Studies, 1984.
4 Lundberg, C.C., 'On the Feasibility of Cultural Intervention in

NOTES

Organisations', in P.J. Frost, L.F. Moore, M.R. Louis, C.C. Lundberg and J. Martin, *Organisational Culture*, Sage: Beverly Hills, 1985.
5 Marsh, P., *Aggro: The Illusion of Violence*, Dent: London, 1978.
6 Lundberg, op. cit.

CHAPTER 4 CROWDS AND EMERGENCIES

1 Moscovici, S., *The Age of the Crowd*, Cambridge University Press: London, 1985.
2 Brook, P., *The Empty Space*, Penguin: Harmondsworth, 1986.
3 Poyner, B., Robinson, D., Hughes, N., Young, M. and Ayles, P., *Safety in Football Stadia: A Method of Assessment*, Scicon: London, 1972.
4 *The Wheatley Report*, HMSO: London, 1972, Cmnd. 4952.
5 Ibid.
6 *Guide to Safety at Sports Grounds*, HMSO: London, 1987.
7 Pauls, J.L., 'Building Evacuations: Research Findings and Recommendations', in D. Canter (ed.), *Fires and Human Behaviour*, Wiley: Chichester, 1980.
8 Fruin, J.J., *Pedestrian Planning and Design*, Metropolitan Association of Urban Designers and Environmental Planners: New York, 1971. See also Pauls, J.L., *Review of Studies of the Movement of People, 1967–1985 by the National Research Council of Canada*, National Research Council of Canada: Ottawa, 1984.
9 *Committee of Inquiry into Crowd Safety and Control at Sports Grounds. Chairman: Mr Justice Popplewell, Interim Report*, HMSO: London, 1985.
10 Tong, D. and Canter, D., 'Informative Warnings: In situ Evaluations of Fire Alarms', *Fire Safety Journal*, 9/3, pp. 267–79, Elsevier: Switzerland, 1985.

CHAPTER 5 COPING WITH VIOLENCE

1 Williams, J., Dunning, E.G. and Murphy, P.J., *Hooligans Abroad*, Routledge & Kegan Paul: London, 1984.
2 Marsh, P., *Aggro: The Illusion of Violence*, Dent: London, 1978.
3 Pearson, G., *Hooligan: A History of Respectable Fears*, Macmillan: London, 1983.
4 Goldstein, J.H. (ed.)., *Sports Violence*, Springer: New York, 1983.
5 Fraser, A., *Cromwell: Our Chief of Men*, Weidenfeld & Nicolson: London, 1983.
6 See *Hansard*, vol. 89, no. 37, p. 234 (16 January 1986), HMSO: London, 1986.
7 Trivizas, E., 'Offences and Offenders in Football Crowd Disorders', *British Journal of Criminology*, 20 (3), pp. 276–88, 1980.
8 Centre for Leisure Research, *Crowd Behaviour at Football Matches: A Study in Scotland*, Dunfermline College of Physical Education: Edinburgh, on behalf of the Football Trust, 19XX.
9 Selbourne, D., 'Through Italian Eyes', *New Society*, p. 395, 14 June 1985.

NOTES

10 Marsh, P., Rosser, E. and Harre, R., *The Rules of Disorder*, Routledge & Kegan Paul: London, 1978.
11 Tiger, L., *Men in Groups*, Nelson: London, 1969.
12 Morris, D., *Soccer Tribe*, Cape: London, 1981.
13 Taylor, I., in R. Ingham, (ed.) *Football Hooliganism: The Wider Context*, Inter-Action: London, 1978.
14 Clarke, J., 'Football and Working Class Fans: Tradition and Change', in R. Ingham (ed.) op. cit.
15 Dunning, E., Murphy, P.J. and Williams, J., 'Spectator Violence at Football matches: Towards a Sociological Explanation', *British Journal of Sociology*, 37(2), 1986.
16 Ibid.
17 Sherif, M., White, B.J. and Harvey, O.J., *Experimental Study of Positive and Negative Intergroup Attitudes Between Experimentally Produced Groups: Robbers Cave Study*, University of Oklahoma: Norman, 1955.
18 Tajfel, H., Billig, M.G. and Bundy, R.P., 'Social Categorisation and Intergroup Behaviour', *European Journal of Social Psychology*, vol. 1, no. 2, pp. 149–78, 1971.
19 *Committee of Inquiry into Crowd Safety and Control at Sports Grounds Final Report. Chairman: Mr Justice Popplewell*, HMSO: London, 1986, Cmnd. 9710.
20 Billig, M. and Cochrane, R., 'The National Front and Youth', *Patterns of Prejudice*, vol. 15, no. 4, pp. 3–15, 1981.
21 Redhead, S. and McLaughlin, E., 'Soccer's Style Wars', *New Society*, 16 August 1985.
22 Morris, T., 'Deterring the Hooligan', *New Society*, 30 May 1985.

CHAPTER 6 THE FINAL SCORE

1 Lee, T.R. and Uzzell, D.L., *The Educational Effectiveness of the Farm Open Day*, Countryside Commission for Scotland: Battleby, Perth, 1980. Prince, D., 'Countryside Interpretation: A Cognitive Approach', *Museums Journal*, vol. 82, no. 3, pp. 165–70, 1982.
2 Pateman, C., *Participation and Democratic Theory*, Cambridge University Press: Cambridge, 1970.
3 Ingham, R., *Football and the Community: Monitoring Report*, Sports Council: London, 1981.
4 Sillitoe, A., 'The Match', in *The Loneliness of the Long Distance Runner*, W.H. Allen: London, 1954.
5 Walvin, J., *The People's Game: A Social History of British Football*, Allen Lane: London, 1975.
6 Downs, D., *Biscuits and Royals: A History of Reading FC 1871–1984*, Fericon Press: Reading, 1984.
7 Canter, D. (ed.), *Fires and Human Behaviour*, Wiley: Chichester, 1980.
8 Ingham, R., op. cit.
9 Uzzell, D. L., *Heritage Interpretation, Volume I: The Natural and Built Environment*, Belhaven Press: London, 1989; Uzzell, D. L., *Heritage*

NOTES

Interpretation, Volume II: The Visitor Experience, Belhaven Press: London, 1989.
10 Tilden, F., *Interpreting Our Heritage*, University of North Carolina Press: Chapel Hill, 1957.

INDEX

advertising 140
aggression, as human trait 110–12
'aggro' 110–12
'animals' 109–10
arrests 14–15, 17, 37, 108
Arsenal 133
attendance 58–63; and conditions 143; drop in 14, 24, 31–48, 129; and grounds 142–3; and identification with club 141–2; and violence threat 14, 137
attitudes 63–4, 74–9; changing 163–5

Baker, Kenneth 159
Billig, M. 119
Bolton disaster 40, 92
bonding: male 110–12; social 116–18
Bradford City fire 94, 98–101, 132
Bristol Rovers 20, 143
British Crime Survey 14
Brook, Peter 86
Brooking, Trevor 160

Cambridge 120
Cameron, A. 105
casualties xviii
catering 149
Celtic 23; attitudes 77–9; conditions 26, 66; support commitment 58
chants 70–2
Charlton Athletic 20, 142–3
Chelsea 23; attitudes 77–9; conditions 66; crowd management 153; racism 72, 119; violence 38–40
Cincinnati Coliseum 88
Clarke, J. 114–15
class, social 113–16

club cultures 9–10, 57–85; attendance and commitment 58–63; attitudes 63–4, 74–9; changing 84–5; 'ethos' 57; grounds 64–70; history 80–2; origins 82–4; racism and fascism 72–4; shouting and swearing 70–2; style of support 70–4; symbols 82
clubs: and community 139, 156–9; identification with 134–5, 141–2; and supporters (*q.v.*) 154–6
Cochrane, R. 119
comfort, spectators' views 24, 26, 65–6
commitment of supporters 58–63
community, and football clubs 139, 156–9
conditions for spectators 24–30, 66, 146–51, 163–5
control 10–13; crowds 12–13, 89, 130–3, 151–4; segregation of supporters 130, 138
Coventry City 23; attitudes 77–9; conditions 66; safety 38; seating 56, 64, 124; support commitment 58; violence 38
cricket 129
crowds 2, 12–13, 86–102, 130; attention focus 87, 130; behaviour 86–7; conflict of interest 94; control 12–13, 89, 130–3, 151–4; crisis legislation 91–3, 132; emergencies 88–90, 98–102; management 12–13, 89; movement 88–90; numbers 88; pedestrian flow 94–8; police presence 90–1; rare events 88, 89; violence 13–18
crushing, spectators' views 40–1

INDEX

culture, football 1–2; club (*q.v.*) 9–10, 57—85
cursing 70–2

data 4–5
Dunning, Eric 103–8, 115–17, 123–6

education 157–9
Edward III, King xiii
Ellis, William Webb xiv
emergencies 12–13, 88–90, 98–102
environmental psychology xv–xvii, 2–5. 128; different perspectives 6–7, 8; survey (*q.v.*) xviii, 6–7; symbolic significance 7–9
'ethos' 57
experts 22–3

families 30
fascism 72–4
flow of pedestrians 94–8
football: authorities 153; club cultures 57–85; crowds 2, 12–13, 86–102; culture 1–2; experience 146–51; history xiii–xv, 105, 161–3; management 146–53; marketing 160; media image 159–61; place of 1–5; popularity 18–19; spectators' views 22–56; violence 2, 13–18, 103–26

Fraser, Antonia 105
Fulham 23; attitudes 77–9; conditions 30, 66; ground 147

General Household Survey 20, 129, 144, 146
Greaves, Jimmy 160
grounds 20–1; closed-circuit TV monitoring 49, 153; and club cultures 64–70; comfort 24, 26; as community resource 20–1, 133–4, 157; improvements to conditions, 24–30, 66, 146–51, 163–5; ownership of 20; safer parts of 41–2, 48; seating 24, 30, 41–2, 48, 56; as symbols 82–3; wasted assets 133–4
Guide to Safety at Sports Grounds 95

Harrison, Paul 115
Heysel Stadium disaster 88, 109, 118–19, 136
Hill, Jimmy 84, 160
hooliganism 14–17; defining 107–9; explanations 109–18; history 104–5;
'new' 120–2; other countries 105–6; other sports 105–6; *see also* violence

IRA 72, 119
Ibrox disaster 40, 89, 92, 136
identification of supporters with clubs 134–5, 141–2
Ingham, R. 139, 156
Inglis, Brian 64
interpretation 162

Japanese Exhibition 88
Jessel, Toby, MP 105
Justinian, Emperor 104–5
Juvenal xiii

'lapsed' supporters 24, 32
legislation 91–3, 132
Leicester University 136
Lundberg, Craig 81–2, 84
Luton 164

McLaughlin, Eugene 120–1
management: caring for supporters 146–51; and cultures 84–5; safety 151–4
Manchester United 23; attitudes 77–9; conditions 66; museum 162–3; souvenirs 150
Manpower Services Commission (MSC) 157–9
marketing football 160
Marsh, Peter 81, 103, 110–12, 121–6
masculinity 115
Maxwell, Robert 142
media image of football 159–61
membership schemes 155–6; spectators' views 48–51
'mickey-taking' 32–3, 76–9
Mill, John Stuart 135
Millwall 23; attitudes 77–9; conditions 26, 66
MORI 14, 20, 144
Morris, Desmond 112
Morris, Terrence 122
movement, crowds 88–90, 94–8
Muranyi, Leslie 120, 122
Murphy, P. J. 103–8, 115–17, 123–6
museums 163

National Front 72, 119
newspapers 4–5; football image 159–61

INDEX

offences; charged 14–15, 17, 37, 108; sentencing 15

Pearson, Geoffrey 103, 120
pedestrian flow 94–8
Peru 41, 106
police 7, 130–2; arrests 14–15, 17, 37, 108; and crushing 41; and legislation, 92–3, 132; presence 90–1
political involvement 72, 118–20
Popplewell Inquiry into Crowd Safety and Control xi–xii, xvi, 49, 51, 100, 105, 120, 152
press 4–5; football image 159–61
Preston North End 23; attitudes 77–9; conditions 66
public relations 159–60

racism 72–4, 119
Ramsey, Sir Alf 109
Reading 142
records of matches 153
Redhead, Steve 120–1
'regular' supporters 24, 32
riots 86, 105–6
Rome, games 104–5
Rousseau, Jean-Jacques 135
Rugby football xiv, 105
rule-systems 11

safety 151–4; management 151–4; spectators' views 37–8, 41–2, 48; *see also* crowds
St John, Ian 160
Scicon 40, 92–3
science 5
Scotland 80
seating 24, 30, 41–2, 48, 56
segregation of supporters 130, 138
self-fulfilling prophecy 11–12
sentencing of offenders 15
Shankley, Bill 19, 164
Sherif, Mustafa 116
shouting 70–2
Sillitoe, Alan 139–40
social representation 138–44
Southampton 23; attitudes 77–9; conditions 66
souvenirs 150
spectators xiv; care for 146–51; conditions for 24–30, 66, 146–51, 163–5; women 20, 143–4; *see also* supporters
spectators' views 22–56; comfort 24, 26;
crushing 40–1; drop in attendance 24, 31–48; experts 22–3; improvements to conditions 24, 26–30; membership schemes 48–51; other teams watched 52; safer parts of grounds 41–2, 48; safety 37–8; supporters 25–6; violence 24–5, 38–40
sponsorship 140
stewards 148–9, 151–2
Sunderland 23; attitudes 77–9; conditions 66; racism 119–20; safety 38
supporters 25–6; attendance and commitment 58–63; care for 146–51; clubs for 155; and football clubs 154–6; identification with clubs 134–5, 141–2; segregation of 130, 138; style of support 70–4; travel to match 148; *see also* spectators
surroundings, symbolic significance of 7–9
survey xviii, 6–7; clubs 23; interviews 24; spectators' views 22–56; supporters 25–6; violence 14
swearing 70–2
symbols of clubs 82–3

Tajfel, Henri 116–17
Taylor, I. 114
Technical and Vocational Education Initiative (TVEI) 157–8
technology: crowd monitoring 49, 153; and crowd safety 93, 101–2
television 3, 19, 129; closed-circuit monitoring 49, 153; football image 159–61
tennis 129
territoriality 112–13
Tiger, L. 111
Tilden, Freeman 162
Tottenham Hotspur 23; attitudes 77–9; conditions 66; shareholders 155; support commitment 63
training, staff 148–9; crowd control 153–4; safety 152–3
travel to matches 148
Trivizas, Eugene 14–15, 108

violence 2, 13–18, 103–26; 'aggro' 110–12; 'animals' 109–10; and attendance 14, 137; and class 113–16; cure 123–4; defining hooliganism

172

INDEX

107–9; explanations 16–17, 109–18; 'new' hooligans 120–2; other times and places 103–7; and politics 118–20; prevention 123; social bonding 116–18; spectators' views 24–5, 38–40; territoriality 112–13; *see also* hooliganism

Waller, Frank 142

Walvin, J. 141
Watford 142, 156–7
Wheatley Report 92–3
White Guide 95
Williams, J. 103–8, 115–17, 123–6
women spectators 20, 144

Youth Training Scheme (YTS) 157

For Product Safety Concerns and Information please contact our EU representative GPSR@taylorandfrancis.com
Taylor & Francis Verlag GmbH, Kaufingerstraße 24, 80331 München, Germany

www.ingramcontent.com/pod-product-compliance
Lightning Source LLC
Chambersburg PA
CBHW050636300426
44112CB00012B/1824